Studies

in

Revelation

Studies in
Revelation

Herman A. Hoyt, Th.D., LL.D.

BMH Books
Winona Lake, Indiana 46590

Dedication

To the many students who have studied this precious portion of the Word of God with me, and have taken courage as the light of His final triumph and soon return have made our hearts to exult together, is this book dedicated.

Cover design: Tim Kennedy
Artwork: Jim Dombek

ISBN: 0-88469-008-3

COPYRIGHT 1966, 1977
BMH BOOKS
WINONA LAKE, INDIANA

Printed in U.S.A.

Preface

The Book of Revelation is all that its name purports. It is a revelation. Learn to speak of it properly. It is not named "Revelations." It is one revelation and should be called "The Book of the Revelation." With equal precision one should think of it as a revelation. It is not a closed book. The second word of the English text, the first in the original Greek, is "revelation." This means that the veil has been taken away, the curtain has been raised, the door has been flung open wide. What was once hidden and sealed is now brought out into the light and made known to men.

The treasure of this crowning book in the pyramid of divine revelation is awaiting the investigation of those who will study it. The lines of truth in the rest of the Bible come to culmination in the Book of the Revelation. Time and effort will be necessary, therefore, to trace out the various lines of truth. And even then it will take time for accumulated facts to merge into a clear picture. Gradually the mighty message of this revelation will burst in floodlight upon the mind and fill the heart with overflowing emotions. Patience is the watchword in studying this book.

A threefold picture of Christ appears in this book in which He is pictured as the absolute and final sovereign of time and eternity. His supreme victory over all His enemies is unveiled to encourage the Bride through the long, long night of wilderness wanderings until He returns to claim His own. Through those years of waiting, the true believer has had to undergo every sort of defamation and persecution; this is intended as the light in the darkness until the day dawn and the Day Star arise in the morning of that eternal day. Today the clouds hang low and the shades of night are deep. But beyond the sunset of this age is that morning when the Sun of Righteousness will rise with healing in His wings.

"He which testifieth these things saith, Surely I come quickly. Amen. Even so, come, Lord Jesus" (Rev. 22:20).

—Herman A. Hoyt

Table of Contents

Preface 5

A Preview of the Book of Revelation 9

1. Introduction to the Revelation of Jesus Christ (chap. 1) 19

2. The Seven Churches of Asia and History (chaps. 2–3) 29

3. The Rainbow-Circled Throne and the Little Book (chaps. 4–5) . 39

4. The Six Seals and the Saved Multitudes (chaps. 6–7) 49

5. The Seventh Seal and the Six Trumpets (chaps. 8–9) 59

6. The Sun-Faced Angel and the Seventh Trumpet (chaps. 10–11) 69

7. The Sun-Clothed Woman and the Dragon (chap. 12) 79

8. The Satanic Trinity in Final Conflict (chap. 13) 89

9. The Zion Vision, the Harvest, and the Seven
   Vials (chaps. 14–16) 99

10. The Doom of the Scarlet Woman and the City of Babylon
    (chaps. 17–18) 109

11. The Marriage in Heaven and the Supper on Earth (chap. 19) . . . 119

12. The Millennium and the Great White Throne (chap. 20) 129

13. New Jerusalem, the Lamb of God, and Eternity
    (chaps. 21–22) 139

Books on Revelation for Further Study 148

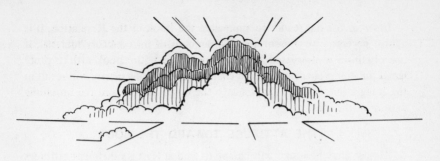

A Preview of the Book of the Revelation

THE CHAPTER OUTLINED:

   I. The Attitude Toward the Book
      1. There are the uninformed
      2. There are the unbelieving
      3. There are the uninterested
      4. There are the unfriendly
      5. There are the untaught
      6. There are the understanding saints

  II. The Name of the Book

 III. The Authorship of the Book
      1. Period
      2. Place
      3. People
      4. Purpose

 IV. The Altitude of the Book

  V. The Approach to the Book
      1. Content of the book
      2. Character of the book
      3. Chronology of the book

 VI. The Outline of the Book

In order for the reader to appreciate the Book of the Revelation, it is almost necessary to present a certain amount of introductory material. If one obtains a well-ordered and full view of the entire book with its problems, the comprehension of each chapter and resulting clarity will result in the integration of each chapter into the larger picture and the unfolding pattern of the ages.

I. THE ATTITUDE TOWARD THE BOOK

Almost anywhere one will be apt to find at least six different attitudes displayed toward the Book of Revelation.

1. There are the uninformed, the vast throng of humanity who know scarcely anything about the Bible, to say nothing about the Book of the Revelation. Being ignorant of its existence, they have no interest in it.

2. There are the unbelieving, that host of people who know about the book but who are not morally inclined or attracted to it. Because it is a part of the Bible, they prefer to have nothing to do with it.

3. There are the uninterested. These will very often be found in the church, preferring to ignore the book as they do other Scripture, but more so perhaps because it is a book of prophecy.

4. There are the unfriendly, too. These are a group of people within the professing church who would rather believe that the book is a compilation of heathen mythologies, fables, fancies, and folklore.

5. There are the untaught, an overwhelming number within the professing church who are interested in the book but who have never been taught at all, or perhaps not rightly taught, or have had no opportunity to be taught.

6. There are the understanding saints. This group is small, of course. They have not only been taught and rightly taught, but have also had a heart to receive the truth and revel in it. May God give all those who read these pages such understanding that their lives will be revolutionized.

This brief analysis reveals only in part the tragedy in Christendom today, especially in the professing church, in the light of what the book says for itself: namely, that it is a revelation, and that this revelation will bring blessing to the people of God (1:1, 3). One preacher is quoted as saying after announcing that he would preach on the book, "I don't know anything, you don't know anything, nobody knows anything about this book." He then closed the book and preached on something else. What tragedy!

II. THE NAME OF THE BOOK

The name you find in your King James Version is "The Revelation of St. John the Divine." Many of the ancient manuscripts carried this title, and from this the translators have carried the name over into the printed Bible. But the title does not belong to the original manuscript written by John. It was added by a later hand. While it is true that John was the writer, it is not his revelation. And while he was a saint of God, he was not divine. However, it must be said that the word "divine" was used in the sense of theologian. The American Standard Version of 1901 carries the title "The Revelation of John." This comes nearer the truth. But the true title is best gleaned from the very first verse of the book, "The Revelation of Jesus Christ." That Jesus Christ gave this revelation to John can be proved by many passages from the book, among which you may consult the following: 1:11-19; 2:1, 8, 12, 18; 3:1, 7, 14; 22:16, 20.

III. THE AUTHORSHIP OF THE BOOK

The authorship of this book is one of the most disputed questions among the scholars of the liberal and semi-liberal school, and the influence of the discussion has had tremendous effect on the conservative school. The one fact that ought to carry more weight than any other is what the book says for itself about its authorship. The solution of this problem covers such matters as the period when this book was written, the place it was written, the people to whom it was written, and the purpose for which it was written.

1. Period. Three dates have been suggested.

(a) The *early date* is A.D. 68-70. It is quite surprising to find that most of the nineteenth and early twentieth century scholars take this position. They do so because they feel the external evidence, though weak, coming as it does from the late fathers of the church, supports it. They feel that the internal evidence from the book itself is very strong in favor of the early date. They think that the contents of the book fit in with the early period of church history in the Roman Empire under Nero. They think they see how the chronology of the book best fits in with this period. And to this they add that the style of language, the various ideas appearing, and the vocabulary used by the writer demand the early period. It can be said here that the whole theological approach these men have to prophecy in general and the Book of Revelation in particular will explain why this attitude is taken. The writer of these pages does not share that theological position.

(b) The *late date* is A.D. 100 or later. This is the conclusion of the liberal school. This position is taken on the basis that the book is not a unity, that many hands have had a part in its writing and editing, with various and sundry turns and twists in the explanations, no two men agreeing. This position falls of its own dead weight even though great scholars have endorsed it. A conservative could not accept it, because it would eliminate John the Apostle as the writer and therefore poses a serious threat to the canon of Scripture.

(c) The *traditional date* is A.D. 95-96. Good scholars hold this view, and practically all of them belong to the conservative school. Moreover, it is reassuring to see this view growing in favor among conservatives. External evidence is very strong. Irenaeus, one of the early fathers, points out specifically when the book was written. And he had direct contact with the Apostle John through Polycarp, who was a disciple of John. Internal evidence can be measured and supported. The chronology of the book fits in with the times of the Emperor Domitian (A.D. 81-96) when there was great persecution of Christians. The tribulation of that time was not universal, nor was it the Great Tribulation of the end time. It was local, that is, here and there throughout the Roman Empire, and to this John makes reference in chapter 1, verse 9. With this period agree the ideas of the book. Most certainly the name of John can be thus explained, for he lived during that period (Rev. 1:1, 4, 9; 21:2; 22:8).

While the character of the Book of the Revelation does differ from the Gospel of John and his epistles, there are very good reasons why this should be true. First, the subject matter is different. Second, the state in which he received this revelation was different. He was "in the Spirit" (1:10), a supernatural state. Third, the style of language was a reversion to his native tongue, Hebrew or Aramaic, because of the great emotional stress he was experiencing. Some have said that his Greek is not good. If so, high emotion would be sufficient explanation. However, one of the greatest Greek scholars of this past generation, Dr. A. T. Robertson, declares that the Greek of the Book of the Revelation is good Greek. Fourth, the source material for the Book of Revelation is almost wholly from the Old Testament (10:7). The reason for this will become more clear as we get into the book. It is because God is beginning to deal again with Israel. Fifth, the symbolism is also almost wholly, if not entirely, from the Old Testament (4:2 and following).

2. **Place.** Two suggestions have been made, and both may fit into one view.

(a)   The *Isle of Patmos* (1:9) was the place the message was received, and it could have been the place where the entire book was written. The word "was" in verse 9 may suggest that John went to Patmos for the vision, but that is already past, and he is now somewhere else as he writes.

(b) The *city of Ephesus* may be the place where this great revelation was finally put into book form for distribution among the churches. It is known that John was finally released from his imprisonment on the Isle of Patmos under Emperor Nerva and returned to the city of Ephesus.

Whether written on the Isle of Patmos or in the city of Ephesus, it is still true that the writing is closely attached to the banishment suffered by John at the hands of the Emperor Domitian, and came near the end of his reign about A.D. 95 or 96.

3. People. There is both an immediate and an ultimate destination for this book.

(a) The *immediate* destination is clearly marked as seven local churches in Asia. Asia does not refer to the continent, or to Asia Minor, but to the westernmost province of Asia Minor. These seven churches had Ephesus for a center in this province of Asia of which Ephesus was the capital (1:4, 11; cf. 2:1, 8, 12, 18; 3:1, 7, 14; 22:9-10, 16). But this is not all.

(b) The *ultimate* destination is marked at the very outset of this book. It is declared that this revelation was given to Christ to show "unto his servants" (1:1). This certainly has reference to Christians in general. This statement does not limit the destination, and therefore it is correct to assume that he includes all believers everywhere. Even the practical applications are always made with this in mind.

4. Purpose. At least a twofold purpose can very easily be discerned in the book.

(a) The first aspect is *predictive.* The revelation is of things which must shortly come to pass. This is to supply people with information of the future (1:1, 3, 19; 10:11; 19:10; 22:10, 18-19).

(b) The second aspect is *practical.* On the basis of information about the future, the purpose is to condition present living with this truth about the future (1:3; 2:7, 11, 17, 29; 3:6, 13, 22; 13:18; 18:4; 19:9; 21:5; 22:6-7, 14, 17).

I trust that every reader of this material will search his own heart and life with this precious truth and see wherein he can live more closely to Jesus Christ than ever before in the light of His soon and imminent return, "for the time is at hand" (Rev. 1:3; 22:10).

IV. THE ALTITUDE OF THE BOOK

This book is the capstone in the great pyramid of divine revelation. Just as Genesis is necessary to explain the origination of all things, so Revelation is necessary to explain the consummation of all things. Without this book the future is almost dark. It is true that other books of the Bible do contain material that is predictive. But none of them open up the future with such a floodlight as does this remarkable book. The important thing to remember is that all the lines of revelation in the entire Bible finally converge in this book. It is therefore important to have a reasonable grasp of the rest of the Bible to understand this book. Many find this book difficult because they are unacquainted with the preceding Biblical material.

V. THE APPROACH TO THE BOOK

The theological viewpoint with which one approaches this book will make all the difference in the world as to what one finds in it. Theological systems are like the blinders on a horse's bridle. They will permit you to see only certain things. Therefore, it is absolutely necessary to study this book under the guidance of a Biblical and valid principle of interpretation.

There are three great schools of interpretation, with many variations of each. For a moment notice what these types of interpretation will do to the contents of the book.

Fictional. This school of interpretation holds that the content of the book is entirely imaginary. Some hold that it is allegorical in form, others that it is parabolical in form, and still others that it is metaphorical in form, but in every case with a spiritual meaning. They argue that certain spiritual principles are stated, illustrated and applied, mostly for encouragement. If this were true, the book could not be a revelation of the future with any power to encourage the saints. People do not usually allow fiction to control their lives to any great extent. It is generally understood that Fact and Form, the meaning of material and the mode of presentation, bear some close relation to each other in order to produce human response.

Historical. This interpretation insists that the material within the book is a record of the facts of history. One group holding to this view argues that everything in the book was completely fulfilled, except chapters 21 and 22, at the time of its writing. Another group holds that everything is being progressively fulfilled in history, except chapters 21 and 22. Unfortunately, the first group leaves God's people today wholly without encouragement, except for the hope of heaven in chapters 21 and 22; while the second group introduce the Christian into a maze of confusion and disorder in the multiplied interpretations they employ to show how chapters 1 through 20 have been fulfilled in the last nineteen hundred years.

Prophetical. This view holds that the book is almost entirely unfulfilled at this present moment, and was even more so in the day when John wrote it. This group holds that chapters 1 to 3 are partially fulfilled; while chapters 4 to 22 are completely unfulfilled. The reasons for taking this position are based on the book itself. The writer holds this view, and the reasons for holding this position are given in brief.

1. Content of the book. The key to the content and analysis of this book is in chapter 1, verse 19. The command comes to John to write about:

(a) Facts of the *past*—"things which thou hast seen" (cf. v. 11). This relates to the vision of Christ (1:12-18).

(b) Facts of the *present*—"the things which are." These are certainly the seven churches "which are" (1:4, 11). Chapters 2 and 3 more clearly describe the churches of that day and through these nineteen hundred years of history.

(c) Facts of the *future*—"things which shall be hereafter." If one compares closely the text of 4:1 with these words of 1:19, he will find there is a very clear connection. The word "hereafter" in the Greek is made up of two words, and rendering it literally it would read, "after these things." The "after this" of 4:1 is the same expression, and also the word "hereafter" of the same verse. "After these things." After what things? After the things that are. Those things are the seven churches. This means after the seven churches have run their course. Beginning with 4:1 to the end of the Book of Revelation the material deals with things which will transpire after the Church has run her course and has been caught up to be with Christ.

2. Character of the book. Several things may be said here that will enable one to understand the nature of this book.

(a) It is *revelation.* This deals with its substance, and to alert us to it, John begins with this word (1:1). God gave it to Christ (1:1), and John recognized it as the word of God (1:9-10), and he was also informed that he was to "seal not the sayings of the prophecy of this book" (22:10).

(b) It is *prediction*. This was true in John's day and remains true two thousand years later. From the point where John stood the future was about to be unfolded (1:1, 19; 10:11; 19:10; 22:6-7, 10, 18-19). The book deals with "things which must shortly come to pass" (1:1).

(c) It is *demonstration*. This refers to the manner in which the revelation was made. The word "shew" in 1:1 appears seven more times in this book (4:1; 17:1; 21:9-10; 22:1, 6, 8). The word means to make a great public display or exhibition.

(d) It is *signification*. Herein is described the means by which this great exhibition is made. The word "signified" of verse 1 means to show by means of signs. So stars, candlesticks, temple furniture, and so forth are used. A "great wonder" appears in 12:1, another in 12:3. John declares in 15:1 that he saw another sign.

(e) It makes *application*. By this the purpose is always kept in view. It reads, "Blessed is he that readeth . . . hear . . . keep" (1:3). Those who do these things clearly demonstrate that they are people who belong to God. They are the kind of people who possess a blessed nature. Those who trifle with these words are described in the closing words of the book (22:18-19).

3. Chronology of the book. The foregoing explanations enable one to divide the book on the basis of the periods of time it treats.

(a) The Period of the Church (chaps. 1–3).

(b) The Period of Tribulation (chaps. 4—19).

(c) The Period of Millennium (chap. 20).

(d) The Period of Eternity (chaps. 21-22).

VI. THE OUTLINE OF THE BOOK

Introduction of the Book (chap. 1)

I. The Revelation of Christ as the Lord of the Churches (chaps. 2–3)
  (Vision of Grace)—Key words: holds, walks, midst (2:1)
  1. The Period of the Apostles (A.D. 30-100) (2:1-7)
  2. The Period of Persecution (A.D. 100-300) (2:8-11)
  3. The Period of Pollution (A.D. 300-500) (2:12-17)
  4. The Period of Catholicism (A.D. 500-1400) (2:18-29)
  5. The Period of Reformation (A.D. 1400-1700) (3:1-6)
  6. The Period of Evangelization (A.D. 1700-1900) (3:7-13)
  7. The Period of Apostasy (A.D. 1900–) (3:14-22)

II. The Revelation of Christ as the Lion over the Nations (chaps. 4—20)

(Vision of Government)—Key word: lion (4:7; 5:5; 10:3; 13:2)

1. The First Half of the Tribulation Period (chaps. 4—11)
2. The Final Half of the Tribulation Period (chaps. 12—19)
3. The Fulfillments in the Millennial Period (chap. 20)

III. The Revelation of Christ as the Lamb Among the Redeemed (chaps. 21—22:5)

(Vision of Glory)—Key word: lamb (21:9, 14, 22-23, 27; 22:1, 3)

1. The Establishment of Eternal Blessedness (21:1-8)
2. The Exhibition of Eternal Blessedness (21:9-27)
3. The Experience of Eternal Blessedness (22:1-5)

Conclusion of the Book (22:6-21)

1

Introduction to the Revelation of Jesus Christ

Revelation 1:1-20

THE CHAPTER OUTLINED:

    I. The Preface of the Book
        1. The nature of the Book of Revelation
        2. The content of the Book of Revelation
        3. The value of the Book of Revelation

   II. The Transition to the Main Theme (vv. 4-11)
        1. The salutation of the book
        2. Now adoration is expressed
        3. The proclamation for the entire book
        4. The situation of the Apostle John

  III. The Person of the Book (vv. 12-16)
        1. The humanity of Christ
        2. The deity of Christ

  IV. The Explanation of the Book (vv. 17-20)
        1. Identification of the speaker
        2. The instruction of verse 19
        3. Valuable information

In this lesson the study will cover the entire first chapter of the Book of Revelation. This chapter is the Biblical introduction to the entire book. Facts and features, signs and symbols, persons and principles appearing herein will provide the student with a guide for understanding the same things that appear later in the book. The reader should make up his mind to study carefully and thoroughly this first chapter, and then determine not to deviate from the meanings reached as he studies the remainder of the book.

For convenience this chapter may be divided into four sections: (1) The preface to the book (vv. 1-3), (2) The transition to the main theme of the book (vv. 4-11), (3) the presentation of the person of the book (vv. 12-16), and (4) the explanation of the content of the book (vv. 17-20).

I. THE PREFACE OF THE BOOK

These opening verses very clearly and concisely point to the nature, content, and value of the book.

1. The nature of the Book of Revelation (v. 1).

(a) It is *revelation*. This describes both its nature and its purpose. The *meaning* of the word "revelation" cannot be overemphasized. It is the first word of the book in the original Greek. It is without the definite article in the Greek, and therefore it lays emphasis upon the nature of the book. It is something revealed: that is, the cover is taken away; there is an unveiling; that which was hidden or concealed is now brought out into the light. Of the Book of Daniel it is declared that its contents were sealed (Dan. 12:4, 9). The seven thunders of Revelation are sealed (Rev. 10:4). But the Book of Revelation is quite the opposite. It is something that is revealed, and as if to remind the reader before he leaves the pages of the book, the angel commands John, "Seal not the saying of the prophecy of this book" (Rev. 22:10). Contrary to the response in many religious circles the opening word ought to attract and not to repel. This word should invite the soul that is hungry for prophetic truth. It should commend the book to any sincere saint of God as something that is open, clear, undisguised, and accessible to the average student of the Word of God. Diligence in the study of this book will result in its yielding up its precious treasure. As it gradually unfolds, the student will be amazed that he did not see this truth before. Thus there will be a progressive confirmation of the meaning of this first word in the heart of the believer.

The *substance* of the revelation, or, to put it another way, the special thing that is being revealed in this book, is "Jesus Christ" (v. 1). The opening words of the book certainly mean that. "The Revelation of Jesus Christ," that is, a revelation concerning Christ, was given by God the Father to the Son, who in turn gave it to an angel to give to the Apostle John. This revelation is especially associated with Christ as the great mediatorial servant and king representing and administering affairs of God in the earth among men. The greater portion of this ministry will begin and continue from the time of His second coming. Of that day and hour, however, Christ did not know. As a true servant, He limited himself on this matter, and it was known only to the Father (Matt. 24:36; Mark 13:32; Acts 1:7). The Book of Revelation is first of all a revelation to Christ, the great servant, and then through Him to the saints of God.

The *source* of this revelation is threefold. Since "God gave" it, God the Father is the ultimate source. Christ receives it "to shew unto his servants," thus making Him the mediating source. The immediate source is the angel, for "by his angel" Christ signified this message to His servant John.

(b) It is *demonstration* as indicated by the word "shew" (v. 1). This depicts the method by which the revelation is made. The original Greek word means public display or exhibition. Careful study of the other seven appearances of the word (4:1; 17:1; 21:9-10; 22:1, 6, 8) suggests that John was made the spectator to the great pictorial drama of the future. This drama consists of "things which must shortly come to pass." Because these things relate to the destiny of the saints, they are sent to Christ's "servants."

(c) It is marked by *signification.* Christ sent and "sign-i-fied" by his angel (cf. 22:16). This means that He used signs to show the meaning of events in the coming Day of the Lord. The agent in carrying out this message by means of signs was an angel. Throughout the book it will be noticed that angels have a great part in making the revelation. This is very much in order inasmuch as angels were before entrusted with great messages from God (Acts 7:53; Gal. 3:19; Heb. 2:2). Such signs as stars, candlesticks, and temple furniture are used (1:20). Old Testament imagery is everywhere in the book (chaps. 10–11).

2. The content of the Book of Revelation (v. 2). John now declares that having received this great message, he performed the function of communicating the revelation. He bore record or testified of "the word of God" and also "the testimony of Jesus Christ." These are not two things. They are but one. In the first John is pointing to God as the source, and in the second he is pointing to Christ as the faithful witness. The American

Standard Version reads in the final clause of verse 2, "even of all things that he saw," thus indicating that this book of revelation is one viewed by an eyewitness, and therefore John is qualified to bear faithful testimony. John is often referred to as a "seer": that is, he saw visions and recorded them. In this sense he belongs to that great class of prophets such as Isaiah, Ezekiel, Daniel and Zechariah. They saw visions and recorded those visions in their writings. John is perhaps the greatest of them all. The Revelation is the record of the most vivid and moving drama of all the ages.

3. The value of the Book of Revelation is very clearly set forth in verse 3. Destination, timeliness, and purpose when joined together give this message high value.

(a) Its *destination* is to three different classes of people. There are those who read, probably the pastors of the congregations. That explains why the singular "he" is used. Books were few in those days, usually only in the hands of pastors, and pastors were expected to be able to read. There are those who hear, that is, those who make up the congregations. There are those who keep the sayings, including both pastors and people. Hearing means hearkening to, showing interest in, and keeping refers to the principle and passion of conforming the life to the patterns and principles of the future.

(b) The *timeliness* of this revelation is suggested by the clause, "For the time is at hand." Two ideas are in this word for time, that of nearness and also that of imminency. Since the word carries with it the idea of time charged with opportunity, how important that God's people know the truth in order that they may be ready for the judgments that will follow.

The full meaning of this word "time" cannot be comprehended without knowing the prophecy of the "70 Weeks" (Dan. 9:24-27). By the time of Christ's first coming the first 69 weeks were fulfilled. But the 70th, the last seven years, was yet future and hidden until the time of the end (Dan. 12:4, 9). At last that time had arrived, and the Book of the Revelation is in large part (chaps. 4–19) the unfolding and elaboration of Daniel 9:27, this final week of years in the history of Israel. That time had arrived 1900 years ago, and today it is 1900 years nearer.

(c) The *purpose* of this book is suggested by the way it ministers blessing. Verse 3 declares, "Blessed is" the one who reads, hears, keeps. It does not say, "Blessed shall be." The word "blessed" does not point to the result of reading, hearing, keeping, but it points rather to what one is in his own nature and character. In other words, those who read, hear, and keep the sayings of this book demonstrate that they are "blessed" people.

Those who love this book and its truth are God's people. They love Christ and His appearing. Their hearts are centered upon the future, the time when Christ will be revealed and exalted among men in the earth. Continuous contemplation of these truths not only brings blessing to them, but this occupation with these truths also enables them to be a blessing to everyone else. This statement is the first of seven such beatitudes in the Revelation (1:3; 14:13; 16:15; 19:9; 20:6; 22:7, 14).

II. THE TRANSITION TO THE MAIN THEME (vv. 4-11)

In a rising crescendo of emotion the writer moves from salutation, to adoration, to anticipation, finally concluding with the situation in which this revelation was given.

1. The salutation of the book (vv. 4-5).

(a) This begins with an *address* (v. 4) which is quite regular. As can be seen, the immediate destination is seven churches of preconsular Asia. They were located in a little province of western Asia Minor, of which Ephesus was the capital. Since these were not all the churches of that region, it must be concluded that they were representative, not just for that period, but for the entire dispensation of grace. The ultimate destination must be all the churches until Christ comes.

(b) The *invocation* of grace and peace (v. 4).

(c) This is followed by naming the *source* of the blessing (vv. 4-5), namely, from the Father, the one "which is, and which was, and which is to come"; from the Spirit, described here in His sevenfold plenitude as "the seven Spirits which are before his throne"; and from Christ, who as prophet is "the faithful witness," as priest is "the first begotten of the dead," and as king is "prince of the kings of the earth."

2. Now adoration is expressed by the Apostle John (vv. 5-6).

(a) He dwells for a moment upon *grace,* as displayed in that supreme act of history and central to the whole ministry of Christ: "Unto him that loveth us, and loosed us from our sins by his own blood" (ASV).

(b) He looks then at *government*, as exhibited in the formation of a spiritual aristocracy for His kingdom, the central feature of which will be mediation between God and men: "And he made us to be a kingdom, to be priests unto his God and Father" (ASV).

(c) He turns finally to *glory,* as pointing to the exaltation of Him who will be the sovereign over all created intelligences throughout the unceasing ages of eternity: "To him be the glory and the dominion for ever and ever. Amen" (ASV).

3. The proclamation for the entire book is now made (vv. 7-8).

(a) It consists of a *prophetic anticipation* of the grand climax of the ages (v. 7). John cannot wait until he gets to that point in the story. He must write it now. This is just a rift in the clouds of judgment, a bit of encouragement for what lies ahead. Here is revelation of the great King. "He cometh with clouds." These are clouds of glory, the proper environment of deity (Dan. 7:13-14). There will be worldwide recognition then. "And every eye shall see him." Through the centuries they knew Him not, but now they recognize Him. And then there will be deep realization on the part of all mankind. "And all kindreds of the earth shall wail because of him. Even so, Amen." This realization will constitute conviction of heart that it was their rejection of Him that culminated in Calvary.

(b) *Divine certification* of the facts in verse 7 are given by the triune God (v. 8). The Father is referred to in the words of verse 4. The Son is described by the words that appear again in 22:13. And the Spirit is included in the words, "Lord . . . the Almighty," which designate the entire Trinity. This should give assurance to the reader that the prediction of verse 7 will ultimately be fulfilled.

4. The situation of the Apostle John is threefold (vv. 9-11). It consists of his geographical location (v. 9), his essential condition (v. 10), and his personal obligation (v. 11).

(a) The *geographical location* of the prophet is "the isle that is called Patmos" (v. 9). It was a little, barren, rock-strewn spot off the coast of Ephesus to which John was banished by decree of the Emperor Domitian. The reason that Roman authorities selected John as a special object for this decree was "for [Greek—'on account of'] the word of God, and for the testimony of Jesus Christ." John was the patriarch and leader of believers in the Roman province of Asia. He lived in Ephesus. He was such a powerful preacher of the Word of God and such a clear witness for the Lord Jesus Christ that it seemed reasonable to destroy John and thus destroy the Christian movement. "In tribulation," as Paul prophesied years before (Acts 14:22), John was a brother and companion with all the saints of his time. Nevertheless, this fellowship included something greater. He was also "in the kingdom and patience of Jesus Christ." Here in this lonely isle John received the greatest revelation ever given.

(b) The *essential condition* of the Apostle John as set forth in verse 10 is in some respects the most important fact in chapter 1. This is a prophetic announcement of that which begins in 4:2, and of which 17:3 and 21:10 are written notations of events along the way. First, note by the word "was" that a change took place in the condition of John. This could be translated more clearly by the word "became." Second, John is thus transferred to a supernatural state, "in the Spirit," literally "in spirit." This means that his normal bodily condition of limitation of time and space has been surmounted, and now in the realm of divine Spirit he is transferred to heaven (Rev. 4:1-2). Moreover, in this condition he is transferred to the Great Day of the Lord, a futuristic period which will be ushered in when the Lord comes and raptures His Church. Read carefully 4:1-2. Here is where this experience begins. In this condition and in this period, John is called to attention by a great voice as of a trumpet (I Thess. 4:16).

(c) A *personal obligation* is now laid upon him by the Lord Jesus Christ (v. 11). It is his responsibility to write down all that he sees and send it to the seven churches of Asia, and ultimately to all the churches during the dispensation of grace.

III. THE PERSON OF THE BOOK (vv. 12-16)

1. The humanity of Christ (v. 13). When John turns to see the voice that speaks with him, he first sees seven golden candlesticks (v. 12), and then one standing in the midst of them. It is Christ's humanity that first comes to his attention.

(a) The *preeminence* of this person is marked by the fact that he stands "in the midst," that is, in the central place and position. He moves continuously in the midst of the candlesticks, or churches (1:20; 2:1), thus symbolizing His continuous and eternal presence in the church (Matt. 18:20; 28:20).

(b) His *resemblance* is "like unto the Son of man." The title or description "Son of man" is taken from Daniel 7:13, and refers to the Son of God become flesh as God's special mediatorial king who will rule in the earth.

(c) In that John sees this vision after Christ went back to glory, and in that it is a vision of something yet future, it is evident that the incarnation of Christ is *permanent*.

2. The deity of Christ (vv. 13-16). From here on the writer is occupied with a description of this person from the viewpoint of His deity.

(a) His *personality* (vv. 13-14) is marked by majesty or greatness in the long flowing robe (cf. Isa. 6:1), by dignity or goodness in the golden girdle with which He is clothed (cf. Isa. 11:5, ASV), and by eternity or duration in the snowy white hair of His head (Dan. 7:9).

(b) His *potentiality* or powers (vv. 14-15) are graphically pictured: His omniscience by "eyes as a flame of fire"; His omnipresence by feet of brass, beautiful and terrible, but set for judgment (cf. John 5:22, 27); His omnipotence by the sound of His voice, with tremendous range from the quiet ripple of the brook to the roar of the ocean (S. of Sol. 2:8, 10; 5:2; Jer. 25:30-31).

(c) His *prerogatives* or rights (v. 16) are symbolized by the right hand and the sword. The right hand marks sovereignty. It is this hand that indicates lordship and control in Scripture (cf. Eph. 1:20). In this right hand is the place of security, protection, safety (John 10:28-29). The instrument of warfare is the two-edged sword proceeding from His mouth. This sword is the almighty Word of God (Heb. 4:12; Eph. 6:17). It is with this sword that Christ fights (Rev. 2:16; 19:15, 21). This is the thing that marks His spirituality.

(d) His *preeminence* is set forth in the vision of His face (v. 16). This is the central feature of this great person. It represents everything He is. Everything else fades into oblivion in its brilliance (Matt. 17:2; Acts 26:13; John 8:12; II Peter 1:19; Rev. 22:16; Mal. 4:2). The light from this countenance is constantly shining (cf. John 1:5; I John 2:8). And its strength or power produces results by destroying the wicked (II Thess. 2:8) and healing the nations (Mal. 4:2).

IV. THE EXPLANATION OF THE BOOK (vv. 17-20)

1. **Identification of the speaker** follows upon the complete physical reaction of the apostle as a result of this amazing vision (vv. 17-18). He is the eternal Son of God, being the first and the last. He is the divine Saviour who lived, died, and lives again. He is the life-giver who satisfied death, and then snatched away the keys to Hades (ASV) so that no child of God would ever go there again.

2. **The instruction of verse 19** is the key to the analysis of the book. The vision of Christ comprises the things he has just seen. The things which are will be set forth in chapters 2 and 3. And the things which will be hereafter begin in 4:1 immediately following the Church Age.

3. **Valuable information** now follows that will enable one to understand the rest of the book (v. 20). The mystery or secret is made known. Stars and candlesticks are explained. Plain things such as the vision of Christ do not need to be explained. Symbols not explained in Revelation are explained elsewhere in the Bible. Unless there is good reason to believe otherwise, everything should be taken as literal. And it may be assumed as

true that more in this book is literal than men are willing to believe.

The stars in the hand of the Son of Man represent angelic creatures in spectacular performance as they exercise custody over the churches. In the Bible stars often represent angels (Job 38:7; Isa. 14:12). They are used by God to minister to His people (Acts 7:53; I Cor. 4:9; Heb. 1:13-14). Angels were appointed over nations (Dan. 10:13; 12:1), so it is quite reasonable that they should be responsible for congregations of believers (Eph. 3:10; I Tim. 5:21; I Cor. 10:11).

The seven candlesticks or lamp stands representing the seven churches mark the number of completeness. Their value is indicated by the material out of which they are made. They are golden, and therefore precious, sacred, the apple of God's eye. They are more than that. To the Son of God they are bone of His bone and flesh of His flesh (Eph. 5:25-33).

The Seven Churches of Asia and History

Revelation 2 and 3

THE CHAPTER OUTLINED:

I. The Interpretation of the Seven Churches
1. During the first century of the Christian Era
2. The portrait of Christ in Chapter 1 and key words
3. Key ideas in the description of Christ
4. At least three interpretations
5. The organization of the material

II. The Exposition of the Churches
1. The church at Ephesus
2. The church at Smyrna
3. The church at Pergamos
4. The church at Thyatira
5. The church at Sardis
6. The church at Philadelphia
7. The church of Laodicea

III. Concluding Observations in This Study
1. Declension
2. As an incentive
3. An entreaty and warning

Chapters 2 and 3 consist of seven very personal letters from Christ to His Church. One letter is directed to each church in particular, and yet in a larger sense that same letter is directed to each of the other churches as well, so that in the fullest sense, the seven letters are directed to the seven churches. This will explain the special destination at the outset of each letter (2:1, 8, 12, 18; 3:1, 7, 14) and the universal application at the close of each letter (2:7, 11, 17, 29; 3:6, 13, 22).

In these letters the sovereignty of Christ over His Church is clearly exhibited. It takes the seven letters and the seven churches to display this in its fullness. Preliminary matters gathering about the essential meaning of these churches require treatment at this point before exposition.

I. THE INTERPRETATION OF THE SEVEN CHURCHES

1. During the first century of the Christian Era and persisting through all these centuries of the Christian church certain *human ideas concerning the supreme authority for the church* have mastered the minds of men. Some have been persuaded that the pastor is the overlord, others the board of elders, still others the official board, yet others the congregation, groups of congregations, denominations, church councils, and even civil government. But any one of these or all of them together form a picture that is inadequate.

2. The portrait of Christ in chapter 1 and key words at the outset of chapter 2 give us the true picture. Christ is pictured as the one who "holdeth" the seven stars. The word describes the exercise of power in the mastery of the stars and, through them, the churches. Christ is also pictured as one "who walketh in the midst" of the seven golden candlesticks (2:1). This means that He occupies the central place of authority and power, and in addition, He is continually attending upon the performance of His functions of oversight.

3. Key ideas in the description of Christ further strengthen the impression of Lordship. Each one of these has already appeared in chapter 1. They are now arranged in relation to the seven churches. In each case the description fits the condition of the congregation and is announced by the Lord himself. "These things saith he that holdeth the seven stars in his right hand, who walketh in the midst of the seven golden candlesticks" (2:1). "These things saith the first and the last, which was dead, and is alive" (2:8). "These things saith he which hath the sharp sword with two edges" (2:12). "These things saith the Son of God, who hath eyes like unto a flame of fire, and his feet are like fine brass" (2:18). "These things saith he that hath the seven Spirits of God, and the seven stars" (3:1). "These things saith he that is holy, he that is true, he that hath the key of David, he that openeth, and no man shutteth, and shutteth, and no man openeth" (3:7). "These things saith the Amen, the faithful and true witness, the beginning of the creation of God" (3:14). No clearer characterizations of Lordship could be presented than these descriptive claims of Christ.

4. **At least three interpretations** prevail concerning the meaning of the seven churches. Sometimes these interpretations are set forth as mutually exclusive. But the facts are against this conclusion. The best solution seems to be that there is real truth in each approach to these churches, and the fullness of the message is to be found only as we recognize that each view merges into the next until completeness is reached. The three interpretations are as follows: historical, typical, and prophetical.

(a) The *historical* interpretation contends that these seven letters were directed to seven local congregations in the province of Asia in western Asia Minor. The statements of the Book of Revelation support this conclusion. Twice reference is made to "the seven churches which are in Asia" (1:4, 11). Twice these seven churches are referred to as "the seven golden candlesticks" (1:13, 20). These seven churches were already in existence, located in cities of Asia, and to them these letters were directed (1:4, 11; 2:1, 8, 12, 18; 3:1, 7, 14). Some of these congregations are named in other portions of Scripture (Eph. 1:1; Col. 4:16). Early church history bears witness to the existence of these churches, and archaeology confirms this testimony. In the writings of the Church Fathers references are made to every one of these congregations, and from the amazing findings of archaeology within recent years every historical point has been verified.

Among commentators there is almost universal agreement on the historical view of these churches. There is at least one notable deviation from this, and that is with Dr. E. W. Bullinger, whose view of the Book of Revelation forced him to his position. He declares that the entire Book of Revelation refers to the future, beginning with the rapture of the church, and therefore these seven churches are not local congregations of the day in which John wrote, but seven Jewish assemblies on earth after the rapture of the Church.

(b) The *typical* approach to the interpretation of the letters to the seven churches is almost equally approved as a necessary and proper method of interpretation. It is the contention of those who hold this view that it is utterly illogical to suppose that the Book of Revelation was written merely to seven local congregations. From other portions of the Book of Revelation itself this seems conclusive (Rev. 1:1; 22:16). But in addition to this, when it is known that there were more than seven local congregations, even in the province of Asia (Col. 1:2; 4:13, 15-16), to say nothing of the dozens existing outside that province, it must be concluded that the number seven must be taken in some typical or perfective sense which includes all other believers.

The number seven has an *ideal sense* denoting perfection or completeness. It pervades the Book of Revelation, appearing at least 53 times, and 11 times in chapter 1. We read of seven Spirits (1:4), seven stars (1:16), seven lamps (4:5), seven seals (5:1), seven horns (5:6), seven eyes (5:6), seven angels (8:2), seven trumpets (8:2), seven thunders (10:3), seven heads (12:3), seven crowns (12:3), seven plagues (15:1), seven vials (17:1), seven mountains (17:9), and seven kings (17:10). The element of completeness or perfection runs through this entire list. It is therefore reasonable to suppose that the same idea is present in the mention of seven churches.

Seven types of congregations seems to be a proper explanation for these seven churches. Beginning with the individual Christian, it is a sensible thing to conclude that there are just seven different kinds. All of these spiritual types can be found in any one congregation. When any one type predominates within a local church, that congregation may be said to be of that type. Since there are only seven types of believers, there can only be seven different types of congregations. Since there were seven different types of believers in each congregation, all the letters had to be sent to each church. And since there were only seven different types of congregations, there was no need for more than seven different letters.

These seven different types *persist* down across the entire stretch of the Christian Era. This is true of individual believers as well as individual congregations. Therefore, the messages to these seven churches are perpetually applicable to all believers. This is an essential corollary to the futurist position that chapters 4 through 22 represent the chronology of events from the rapture of the Church on. If the seven churches were merely historical congregations of John's day, from the viewpoint of the 20th century there is a break in the chronology of almost 1900 years. The typical view of these churches, therefore, helps to bridge the gap between the historical churches of John's day and the period ushered in by the coming of Christ for the Church. "Hereafter" and "after this" of 1:19 and 4:1, marking the movement of chronology from the churches to the tribulation period, present an unbroken process in the unfolding of the purposes of God in history.

(c)   The *prophetical* interpretation seems to be an almost certain conclusion to the futuristic approach to the Book of Revelation. This view insists that the seven spiritual types of congregations also picture a progressive unfolding of the condition of the church in seven successive stages of its history. Even though all spiritual types will persist throughout the entire history of the church, in the very nature of the case, as different types of believers will predominate in the various local congregations, so also will different types of congregations come to predominate in the various stages in the process of the church. This can only mean that seven spiritual stages will eventually develop in the progressive unfolding of the church through the entire history of her sojourn here in the earth.

This conclusion is *demanded* by the meaning given verse 19 of chapter 1. If this verse is the key to the analysis of the book, then "the things which are" refer to the churches, and "the things which shall be hereafter" refer to events from chapter 4 on. This coincides with the statements in 4:1, and seems to agree so perfectly because the letters to the seven churches have been written (chaps. 2–3). "After this" and "hereafter" of 4:1, which literally means "after these things," must refer to what has already preceded, namely, the churches. If this be true, then one must insist that chapters 2 and 3 are more than letters to seven historical churches, for this would leave a chronological break of almost 1900 years as viewed from the present time. If the typical interpretations bridge this gap, then it is also reasonable to believe that this gap is bridged in some orderly procedure. This is the prophetical explanation of these seven churches.

There are vigorous *opponents* of this view among those who take the futuristic approach to this book. They take opposition because they want to preserve the precious truth of the imminent return of Christ for the Church. This is understandable if the point of emphasis in the prophetical view is to outline the chronology of the seven successive stages in church history from the beginning of the Christian Era. This would be just another clever scheme for setting the date for the coming of Christ and destroying the precious truth of the imminent return of Christ. The writer joins in opposition to any such handling of the prophetical interpretation of these churches. But there is a more judicious way to treat this method of interpretation, and one which is not only Biblical but also gives the imminence of Christ's return its proper place in prophetic truth.

The *character* of this book is announced in its opening words so far as its content is concerned. It is to deal with "things which must shortly come to pass" (1:1). This certainly gives predictive quality to everything which follows, and this would include chapters 2 and 3. But this must be written to churches that exist in order to preserve the truth of Christ's imminent return. However, hidden within the historical is the predictive element that emerges into seven periods in the unfolding history of the church.

Since the *history* of the church is living and dynamic, sharp lines of demarcation between periods cannot be drawn. This will be an ever chang- ing pattern until the church has at last run its course. The transition from one period to another is gradual, merging, and imperceptible. But the responsibility to discern the trend of the times and conform the life to the facts of the imminent future remains.

The following *scheme* of prophetic interpretation is proposed without insisting that there is anything hard and fast about the divisions. The designation of each church seems to fit a period in history. Ephesus means "desirable" and fits the apostolic period from A.D. 30 to 100. Smyrna means "myrrh," an herb that gives forth fragrance when it is crushed. This answers to the period of persecution from A.D. 100 to 300. Pergamos signifies being thoroughly married. This describes the period of the union of Church and State from 300 to 500. Thyatira carries the sense of con- tinuous sacrifice and depicts that period when Catholicism dominated all professing Christendom from 500 to 1400. Sardis means "remnant" and answers to the Reformation period from 1400 to 1700. Philadelphia de- notes brotherly love and suggests the time of missionary movement and evangelization from 1700 to 1900. Laodicean means "judgment of the people" and is closely akin to the word democracy. It represents that period of growing apostasy from 1900 on.

5. **The organization of the material** in each of the seven letters follows a rather well-defined pattern. At the outset of each epistle the *destination* is given. This is followed by a *description* of the author, which always fits the spiritual condition of the church. From these facts the *dispensation* of the church is set forth, the name and condition of the church indicating this. The *diagnosis* is clearly set forth, sometimes good, sometimes bad, sometimes both. There is usually a *demand* laid upon the church consisting of a command from the Lord to repent and reform. A *dynamic* is always provided for individual believers to overcome. In every letter a word of *discrimination* appears. This is for the purpose of sifting out the wheat

from the tares.

II. THE EXPOSITION OF THE CHURCHES

In this discussion the diagnosis alone will be treated.

1. The church at Ephesus (2:2-4, 6).

(a) This was an *evangelistic* church. It had "laboured" (vv. 2-3). In its early zeal no stress or strain was too great, no trial or tribulation too appalling, no heartache, misunderstanding, misfortune was enough to dampen its ardor and enthusiasm for souls.

(b) This was a *separated* church. It could not "bear them which are evil" (v. 2). Discipline was exercised in the church. People were excommunicated for worldliness, and in this way the church was kept clean, and many were turned away from their sin.

(c) This was an *orthodox* church. It "tried them which say they are apostles, and are not, and hast found them liars" (v. 2). Infidelity to the truth among the leadership or feigned leadership was not tolerated. As a result false doctrine did not get any real foothold in that early century.

(d) This was a *laymen's* church. Christ says, "But this thou hast, that thou hatest the deeds of the Nicolaitanes, which I also hate" (v. 6). The word "Nicolaitanes" means "conquerors of the people." It was a group who argued that there are two classes in the professing church, clergy and laity. Of course, it was the clergy who ruled over and dominated the laity. However, Christ hated such division, as also did this church. The ministry of the church is not to one class above others. It, as a class, is simply given gifts for a particular purpose, even as others are given gifts to perform other functions.

(e) This church has lost its *"first love"* (v. 4). The emotional fervor with which this Early Church had been joined to the great Bridegroom had disappeared at the close of the first century. The spontaneity and expectancy with which this church had hurried about its duties and momentarily looked for the return of the Bridegroom faded into a work-a-day drudgery and loyalty. Except in remote and isolated places that first love has been absent in the professing church now for more than 18 centuries. The animated activity which arises out of a jubliant expectancy of the coming of the Lord is still a strange thing in most of Christendom.

2. The church at Smyrna (2:9).

(a) It was an *energetic* church, full of works.

(b) It was a church that had to endure great *persecution*.

(c) As a result, great *poverty* came upon the people. They were driven from their homes; their goods were confiscated; their businesses were boycotted. All of these things were to their credit.

(d) But of all things, there crept into this church those who claimed to be Jews and were not. Actually they were of the synagogue of Satan. By their Judaizing tendencies and legalistic measures they were guilty of blaspheming God.

3. The church at Pergamos (2:13-15).

(a) This was a *presumptuous* church. Instead of fleeing from the world and satanic influence, it had actually taken up its dwelling "where Satan's seat is" (v. 13).

(b) But it was still a *fundamental* church, not denying the faith of Christ even in the face of severe martyrdom, such as Antipas experienced (v. 13).

(c) However, the *leavening* of the church had begun. The doctrine of Balaam was being spread by a few (v. 14). This doctrine removed the clear line of demarcation between the church and the world and eventually resulted in the union of church and world.

(d) Here the seeds of *Nicolaitanism* begin to thrive (v. 15). The clergy class begin to emerge in the church, and unlike the Ephesian church, this church does not hate the group who holds this teaching.

4. The church at Thyatira (2:19-21).

(a) This church is characterized by *externalism.* In it there is great organization, orthodoxy, and socialization (v. 19). Multiplication of forms, many statements of faith, enlarged social service, incessant activity are there.

(b) Yet on the inside its life was being sapped by *Jezebelianism* (vv. 20-21). This was a mixture of Christianity, Judaism, and paganism. Spiritual fornication was being practiced, and though, through the reformers, God made an effort to get this church to repent, it is unrepentant to this day.

5. The church at Sardis (3:1, 2, 4).

(a) This is a church with great *reputation* (v. 1). But in spite of its reputation it is generally inactive in Christian things, and dead. Any close examination of the Reformation church will reveal that it made great claims to orthodoxy, but its piety was very low, and there was little or no general movement in evangelization.

(b) Even in this church there was a *remnant* (vv. 2, 4). These were faithful and active, and by their efforts the remaining few, though ready to die, were strengthened.

6. The church at Philadelphia (3:8-10).

(a) This is a *conservative* church (v. 8). Because of its stand for the faith, there was an open door of opportunity for evangelism.

(b) Here also was *cleanliness* of life (v. 9). God made this church His first exhibit to Catholics and Protestants alike that grace, not law, is the way to produce piety. With purity of doctrine there comes purity of life.

(c) To this church God promises *protection* from the trial that is to come upon the earth (v. 10). This time of trial is the period of great tribulation.

7. The church of Laodicea (3:15-17, 20).

(a) This is a *worldly* church and decidedly lukewarm (vv. 15-16).

(b) It is a *wealthy* church so far as earthly possessions are concerned (v. 17).

(c) It is a *wretched* church, without feeling or mercy (v. 17).

(d) It is a *weak* church, poor, blind, naked, when looked at from the spiritual standpoint (v. 17).

(e) Worst of all, it is a church *without Christ.* He stands outside the door (v. 20). You will notice that the address is different from those to the other churches. This letter is written to the church of the Laodiceans. The people have taken over here, and since they "have need of nothing" (v. 17), not even Christ, of course He stands outside.

III. CONCLUDING OBSERVATIONS IN THIS STUDY

1. Declension in the church through the entire Church Age finally reaches its worst in the Laodicean church. In devotion it begins with a loss of first love at Ephesus and reaches the stage of lukewarmness. In doctrine it begins with legalism at Smyrna and finally pushes the Lord out altogether. In duty it begins with worldly union at Pergamos, mounts up to general inactivity, and finally becomes completely inactive. In defilement it begins with unholy union with the world at Thyatira and finally descends to the place where the church has lost her white garments and is utterly naked.

2. As an incentive through the Church Age the Lord holds out the promise of reward to the overcomer (2:7, 11, 17, 26-28; 3:5, 12, 21).

3. An entreaty and warning is also given to every professing believer (2:7, 11, 17, 29; 3:6, 13. 22).

The Rainbow-Circled Throne
and the Little Book

Revelation 4 and 5

THE CHAPTER OUTLINED:

1. Arguments from silence
2. Arguments from analogy
3. Arguments from doctrine
4. Arguments from Revelation

I. The Setting of the Throne (Chap. 4)
1. The introduction
2. The throne
3. The elders
4. The beasts
5. The worship

II. The Preparation of the Throne (Chap. 5)
1. The little book
2. The Lion-Lamb
3. The creation-praise
4. Some important questions

As the study now enters the fourth chapter, the *next major movement* in the unfolding of the prophetic program is before the student. In this division of the book there is a revelation of Christ as the Lion over the nations. The dispensation of grace is past, the Church has been caught up to heaven, and the Day of the Lord has been ushered in. In this portion of the book, chapters 4 through 20, the reader gets a vision of divine government. The Lion of the tribe of Judah is now dealing with the earth (Rev. 5:5). He rules with the rod of iron (12:5). He comes in wrath to deal with the wicked (19:15). And He finally establishes His kingdom, the first movement of which is for 1000 years (20:6); at the end of that time it merges into the everlasting reign (22:5).

There is grave need for establishing the fact that the *rapture of the Church* takes place at the close of chapter 3. The following arguments do not exhaust the subject.

1. Arguments from silence. It needs to be remembered that the rapture of the Church is a family affair and not a public event. This event is to include every member of the Church during the whole period of grace. It would therefore have been impossible to declare it at the end of chapter 3 without conveying the impression that only the members of the seven churches were meant, and without also taking away the imminency of that event. It must also be remembered that there is no mention of the Church on earth throughout the entire tribulation period covered by chapters 4 through 19. And certainly no other passage of Scripture declares that the Church will pass through the terrible period of tribulation.

2. Arguments from analogy. What has happened to others in the past, who stand in some small way as types of the Church, suggests that the Church is raptured away before the tribulation period. Enoch and Lot were transferred away from the scene of judgment (Gen. 5:24; 19:21-24), and believers are promised that they will not come into judgment (John 5:24). The Apostle John is certainly representative of the Church, and he is invited to "come up hither" just before the tribulation period begins (Rev. 4:1-2).

3. Arguments from doctrine. It is definitely asserted in Scripture that the Christian cannot come into penal judgment, and certainly the tribulation is a period of judgment (John 5:24; Rev. 4:2; 14:7). Therefore it is only logical to argue that believers will not pass through this period of wrath upon the earth (Rom. 5:9; I Thess. 1:9-10; 5:9; Rev. 6:16-17). This is consistent with the clear teaching of the Word of God that believers should look for the coming of the Lord at any moment, which would be nullified if the events of chapters 4 through 19 must first come to pass (cf. Luke 12:35-47; Titus 2:13).

4. Arguments from Revelation. There are no better arguments to establish the transition from the Church Age to the period of tribulation, between chapters 3 and 4, than those which come from the book itself. And no one has more right to speak with authority on this point than the Apostle John, who wrote the book.

(a) The sequence of time marked by the book itself indicates that the Church has already been caught up to glory. There is no mistaking the movement of things as declared by Christ in chapter 1, verse 19. The things John had already seen were the vision of chapter 1. "The things which are" refer to the seven churches mentioned in chapter 1, verse 4, 11 and chapters 2 and 3. And "the things which shall be hereafter" must be the things that begin with chapter 4. "Hereafter" is literally "after these things." Twice in chapter 4, verse 1, the same words appear. "After this" and "hereafter" cannot mean anything other than what the same words mean in chapter 1, verse 19, namely, after the Church things or Church Age is passed.

(b) The first vision of Christ is among the churches, but in chapters 4 through 19 Christ is in heaven (cf. 1:13 with 4:1-2; 5:5-6). This certainly suggests that the Church is also with Him (John 14:1-3).

(c) The promise made to the Philadelphian church was that it would be kept from the hour of trial (Rev. 3:10). It is only logical to believe that this promise will be fulfilled for all church saints, and in chapter 4 has already taken place.

(d) The Church is pictured as being in heaven during the tribulation period. In Revelation 13:6 (ASV) it is declared that Antichrist opens his mouth in blasphemies against God, "to blaspheme his name, and his tabernacle, even them that dwell in heaven." Surely no other than the Church can be called God's tabernacle (cf. Eph. 2:21 with Rev. 3:12). Then when we get to Revelation 19:1, 7-8 there is the bride in heaven prepared for the wedding of the Lamb (cf. II Cor. 11:2).

(e) When Christ comes in glory, His saints, the Church, come with Him from heaven to the earth (Rev. 19:11-21. If the calling up of John in Revelation 4:1 is representative of the rapture of the Church, and then the coming of Christ with His saints in glory in Revelation 19:11-21 marks their return to the earth, then surely throughout the entire tribulation period the Church is in heaven and not upon the earth.

(f) In the opening vision of the fourth chapter, 24 elders are seen around the throne. These must represent the Church (Acts 20:17 and following; James 5:14; Rev. 4:4). Elders represent the Church today, and no better symbol could be used in this vision. They are seen in heaven throughout the entire tribulation period (4:4, 10; 5:5-6, 8, 11, 14; 7:11, 13; 11:16; 14:3; 19:4). After the marriage of the Lamb, when Christ returns to earth with His Church, the elders are never seen again. The reason lies in the fact that the Church is with Him and there is no need for representation (cf. Rev. 20:4-6 with 2:26-27; 3:21).

The *chronology* of chapters 4 through 20 can be very easily charted. The beginning of the tribulation period of seven years is marked in 4:1. The middle point of the tribulation is indicated in 11:2-3, 15. The end of the tribulation period is brought about by the coming of Christ (Rev. 19:11-21). The Millennium and its course are described in chapter 20.

Chapters 4 and 5 constitute the introductory vision to the events which will happen in heaven and earth during the entire tribulation period. The vision, however, is a scene largely staged in heaven. Chapter 4 consists of the description of the throne of judgment for the tribulation period, while chapter 5 pictures the preparation of the throne for judgment.

I. THE SETTING OF THE THRONE (Chap. 4)

1. The introduction (vv. 1-2). The *passing* of the Church Age is indicated by the words "after this," "hereafter" (Greek—"after these things"; cf. 1:19). The *promotion* of the Church into heaven is suggested by the experience of John when he sees the door opened in heaven, hears the trumpet voice of Christ (1:10, 12), responds to the call, "Come up hither," and listens to the promise of seeing things which will come to pass after the Church is raptured. The *procession* of events following the Church Age is set forth by the words "things which must be hereafter," or more literally from the original Greek, "things which it is necessary to come to pass immediately after these things." History does not come to an end with the rapture of the Church.

2. The throne (vv. 2-3, 5). The words "was set" or, more literally, "was sitting" indicate that this throne is the permanent throne of God. The imperfect middle voice of this verb is used as in John 2:6 in the sense of denoting a continuation of the throne. This marks its absolute sovereignty, undisturbed by movements of men or events, unperturbed by sin and rebellion among creatures. Up to this time the throne of God has been working all things after the counsel of His own will (Eph. 1:11), exercising grace and patience and long-suffering toward wicked and gainsaying men.

All this has been possible because "known unto God are all his works from the beginning of the world" (Acts 15:18). But now the time has arrived for new activity from this throne. Chapters 4 and 5 give a description of heavenly arrangement in preparation for earthly administration. The earthly administration will follow in chapters 6 through 19. Afer millenniums of time in which men have finally convinced themselves that there is no God of judgment, perhaps no God at all, God in His own time begins a new activity from the eternal throne. Therefore the eternal throne of God is now taking on aspects for the specific purpose of judgment.

The *person* on this throne is not named. We read merely that "one sat on the throne" (v. 2). The person is indescribable except for the fact that He is like a jasper and a sardine stone (v. 3). From the thrice repeated "holy" of verse 8, it may be concluded that this is the triune God.

The *purpose* of the throne at this point may be described as that of adjudication, to mete out judgment on the basis of the law (v. 5) and to extend mercy and salvation in the midst of judgment as suggested by the "rainbow round about" (v. 3).

The *procession* from the throne of "lightnings and thunderings and voices" (v. 5) indicates that God is going to deal with the earth on the basis of the law from Sinai (cf. Exod. 19:16; Luke 16:29-31).

3. The elders (v. 4). The *identity* of these elders is not easy, although they seem to represent the Church. Just as 24 elders represented the 24 courses of priests in Israel (I Chron. 24:3-5), so also 24 elders represent the Old Testament saints and 12 the New (Rev. 21:12-14). But this is unlikely for the very specific reason that the Bible seems to teach that the Old Testament saints are not resurrected from the dead until the end of the tribulation period (Isa. 26:19-21). Even after they are resurrected they are never raptured into heaven, but live to rule and reign with Christ during the kingdom (Dan. 12:1-2; Rev. 20:4). The *garments* of "white raiment" point to the righteousness of the saints in which they are now clothed (Rev. 3:5; 19:7-9). These are *thrones* and not mere seats upon which they sit. Authority for judging, ruling, reigning has been committed to them (Rev. 5:10; 20:4-6; I Peter 2:5-9). *Crowns* upon their heads tell the story of victories gained as they lived the overcoming life in the earth (Rev. 2:26-27). These are not diadems, but the sort of crowns given to victors.

4. The beasts (vv. 6-8). The *identity* of the beasts is important. The American Standard Version gives a better rendering, calling them "living creatures." They represent God in governmental relation to all created life upon the earth. In Ezekiel 10:20 they are called cherubim. The *variety* suggests that they have power to assume different forms to symbolize different truths. The lion signifies divine majesty; the ox, divine strength; the man, intelligence and purpose; the eagle, swiftness in detecting evil and executing judgment; while the wings and eyes signify incessant activity and omniscience. The locality of these four creatures (v. 6) "in the midst . . . and round about" the throne suggests properly their relation to the one who is on the throne. They represent the various attributes of God in His providential control of the universe. The *activity* of these creatures, the fact that "they rest not day and night" (v. 8), suggests how ceaselessly they perform the tasks they were created to perform. Apparently one task is to give praise to the triune God.

5. The worship (vv. 9-11). The *occasion* for the worship of the elders is the glory given to God by the four living creatures (v. 9). Incited by the adoration of the creatures, the 24 elders are not less *demonstrative* in theirs (v. 10). They fall before the throne, showing their wonder; they worship, showing adoring hearts; they cast their crowns won in victory before Him, for, after all, the crowns belong to God. The *ascription of praise* from the hearts of the elders is the realization of the great plan and purpose of God in creating and redeeming men (v. 11).

II. THE PREPARATION OF THE THRONE (Chapt. 5)

1. The little book (vv. 1-4). The key to the understanding of all that follows rests in the *identification* of this book (v. 1). The popular idea is that this book is one revealing events that are to follow. Some have suggested that it is the history of the church; others, the covenant with Israel that is yet to be made. In those days, books were not leaf-backs, such as we have today, but scrolls. This book was written on both sides. It was rolled a little way and a seal was placed on it. It was rolled a little more and another seal was placed on it. Finally it was completely rolled up and seven seals secured it.

Archaeology has brought to light a similar little book. It was stored away in an earthen vessel for safekeeping. When examined it was found to be a title deed to a piece of property, and the seals were the official stamp of authority and protection upon it. But the Bible can interpret itself. Every student of this portion of Scripture should study carefully Jeremiah 32:6-16, wherein a similar book was inscribed and sealed by Jeremiah, giving him the official right to property he purchased just before the invasion of Nebuchadnezzar. Such is the book before us in this chapter. It is the title deed to the universe. The removing of the seals will be steps in

taking possession of the purchased property. These steps, of course, constitute a movement of events. And in this sense there is a relation of the
future. But the primary meaning of the little book is that of a title deed.

The *importance* of this little book cannot be overestimated (vv. 2-3).
An intensive search is instituted to discover a man who can open this
book. But though heaven and earth and the nether world are searched, no
man is found. In fact, the original text says that no creature of any kind
was found worthy to open the book. By sin Adam had forfeited his right
to open it, and all his descendants are in the same position. Nor do angels
have any right to open this book. Only the owner of the property and the
one who redeemed it has that right. But he has not been found.

The intense *interest* displayed in this book is exhibited by John when
he bursts into tears (v. 4). He weeps as one would weep at a funeral for
one who passes on and will never return. The devil and his hosts are in
possession of the earth and its environs. They have usurped it and will
remain in possession of it until the rightful owner comes and expels them.
The overwhelming thought that there is none to open the book, and such a
one may never be found, crushes John with grief.

This expression of grief on the part of John is representative of the grief
felt by the people of God throughout history. With Satan in control of
God's earth the wicked have prospered while the righteous suffer. This was
the problem before Habakkuk as he wrote his prophecy. It has ever posed
a baffling puzzle to the saints. If righteousness is right and God is a God of
judgment, then where is the God of judgment? Why does He hesitate to
destroy the wicked and deliver the righteous? Can it be that at this strategic moment when the title deed to the universe is displayed, the rightful
owner cannot be found to take possession and expel the usurpers? The
thought overwhelms John with disappointment and despair, and all his
lifelong hopes seems to be dashed to pieces.

2. The Lion-Lamb (vv. 5-7). But even while John is shaken with uncon-
trollable disappointment and despair, one of the elders points out to him
the fact that the Lion of the tribe of Judah has qualified himself to open
that book (v. 5). John lifts his head and looks at the throne, and in its
midst he sees a Lamb, one that has been slain and has the marks of the death
wound still upon it. This is none other than the Lion (Gen. 49:10) from
between the feet of Judah, and the root of David, his greater Son (Isa.
9:6-7); He is here identified as the Lamb of God, who at the cross redeemed the universe and is now constituted with authority to open the
title deed.

John does not realize, much less others, how far-reaching and important the death at the cross really is. It accomplished the redemption of mankind. But few realize that this redemption also extends to the universe. Somehow, when sin entered the universe through creatures, it affected everything. Therefore it was necessary for redemption to cover the place of man's abode as well as himself. In this passage it is evident that the efficacy of Christ's death extends to the universe as well as to mankind.

Now the most dramatic event of the ages takes place. "And he came and took the book out of the right hand of him that sat upon the throne" (v. 7). There is the focal point of all the ages. With a ruined earth in the hands of Satan, yet potentially redeemed, with a waiting host looking forward to the actual expulsion of the usurpers and the taking of possession, John watches intently to see what will happen. The Lamb steps up and takes the book firmly in His grasp, never to release it again. The act is supercharged with suspense.

3. The creation-praise (vv. 8-14). *Redeemed creation* now bursts forth into an ecstasy of delight and a paean of praise (vv. 8-10). From the midst of the throne and immediately around it, the four living creatures, representing all creation, begin this praise. The elders, representing the church, from their seats about the central throne catch it up and carry it into a widening circle. Though the rendering of the American Standard Version at this point intimates that the living creatures and the elders may be speaking of others, it is fairly certain that comparison with Revelation 1:6 and 20:6 establishes its validity for them. Since this redemption applies to many beyond themselves, they are merely including others with themselves by using the third person. *Angelic creation* then catches up the song of ecstasy as the praise spreads to an ever-widening circle of creation (vv. 11-12). Then *remaining creation* is progressively swept into the intoxicating surges of emotion and praise (vv. 13-14).

The chronology of this event is disturbing to many. But if it is remembered that this is a vision that carries through to the end, it will help the reader. The praise begins in heaven when Christ takes the book into His hands. It progresses until all heaven has joined in the song. It sweeps to the earth at the opening of the Millennium when Christ takes over the rule, and continues to grow until at last, when the eternal state has been ushered in, all creation has joined in this glad song. There is reason to believe that once it begins it will never end.

4. Some important questions now receive an adequate answer. Some wonder why God permitted sin in the beginning. The answer seems to be that He permitted sin to enter the universe that His grace might finally bring universal praise. As John the Apostle, many want to know why God delays judgment when it is so much deserved. The answer again seems clear. Delaying judgment makes it possible for a full harvest of saved on the one hand, while giving time for the wicked to come to full ripeness for judgment, on the other hand, thus proving irrefutably that God must intervene in human affairs. The delaying of judgment also proves the absolute faithfulness and all-sufficiency of the infinite and gracious God.

· 4

The Six Seals
and the Saved Multitudes

Revelation 6 and 7

THE CHAPTER OUTLINED:

       1. Progressive movement

       2. Successive movement

I.   The Opening of the Six Seals (Chap. 6)

       1. Introduction

       2. Exposition

II. The Saving of Two Multitudes (Chap. 7)

       1. The sealed servants

       2. The saved saints

Two literary devices are employed in chapters 6 through 19 for the purpose of unfolding clearly the movement of events covering the seven-year period of tribulation. These comprise three series of sevens—seven seals (6:1-17; 8:1), seven trumpets (8:2–9:21; 11:15-19), and seven vials (15:1–16:21)—and nine insets in as many chapters (chaps. 7, 10, 11, 12, 13, 14, 17, 18, 19).

The *three series of sevens* mark the movement of history from the moment the tribulation period is ushered in to its close. Some Bible students have taught that these seven seals, seven trumpets, and seven vials are merely seven different ways of saying the same thing; hence the first seal, the first trumpet, and the first vial all describe the same event, and so on for the rest. Such a position is difficult to sustain from the record itself. For this reason, note carefully several points that will support the position that three groups of seven are successive and not simultaneous at the point of time they are initiated. Once the events are initiated many run concurrently.

1. The progressive movement of events in the history of the tribulation period from the moment it begins until its close is being portrayed. The seals come first and move one by one to the seventh (6:1-17; 8:1). With the opening of the seventh seal, the seven angels with the seven trumpets come into view (8:1-2). These trumpets are blown one by one through the seventh (8:7–9:21; 11:15-19). Then another series comes into view, namely, the angels with the vials (15:1, 7-8; 16:1-21), and these are called the last.

2. The successive movement of events in this history of the tribulation period is clearly marked by words describing time relation. After the first seal is opened, each successive seal is indicated by the use of the ordinals—second, third, and so forth (6:3; 5, 7, 9, 12; 8:1)—and the same also for the trumpets (8:7-8, 10, 12; 9:1, 13; 11:15) and the vials (16:1-3, 8, 10, 12, 17). The seven trumpets follow the opening of the seventh seal (8:1-2), and the seven vials are said to be another in the succession of signs (15:1).

3. There is increasing intensity of the judgments from the seals through the vials. There is a growing intensity of judgments in the seals, so that when the sixth is reached men have a premonition of the coming day of wrath (6:15-17); with the opening of the seventh even heaven is hushed into silence (8:1), because it opens up the seven trumpets of judgment. The final three trumpets are called woes (8:13) because they are so much more severe than the first four. The vials exceed even the trumpets, because in them are the seven last plagues in which "is filled up the wrath of

God" (15:1). This growing intensity has the very practiced effect of demonstrating that men are confirmed in their sin and beyond the reach of the grace of God.

The *nine chapters containing insets* depict features in the movement of history during the tribulation period that logically come into view at the point where they are introduced, but their history reaches backward and also forward. For instance, chapter 7 describes two groups who will be saved during the tribulation period, the first group during the first half, and the second group during the last half. Chapter 13 traces the history of Antichrist from his rise to the height of his career.

THE OPENING OF THE SIX SEALS (chap. 6)

1. Introduction.

(a) The *setting* for the opening of the seven-sealed book has already been made (chap. 5). The Lion of the tribe of Judah, the Lamb of God, has prevailed to open the book, the title deed to the universe; and He has assumed His authority, stepped to the throne, and taken the book into His hands. All created intelligences of heaven and earth wait expectantly for the performance of those dramatic events when Christ shall tear away the seals and take possession of His universe. Let it be remembered that Christ holds the title deed, and He is the only one qualified to open the seals, and that He is the one who opens the seals. It must also be remembered that He is in heaven as He opens the seals. This means that He directs the course of judgment from heaven and does not return personally to the earth until the end of the tribulation period (Rev. 19:11-21).

(b) The *series of seals* is opened in strictly chronological order. How much time elapses between each one is not known, but it does seem that they move swiftly, so that the seventh is opened by the middle of the first half of the tribulation. Moreover, there seems to be a slight difference in the seven. The first four, the four horsemen, deal with the earth; while the last three portray scenes that bring heaven more largely into view. The first seal is broken, the scroll is unrolled, and judgment goes forth. The second seal is broken, the scroll is unrolled a bit farther, and another judgment proceeds. This goes on until all seven seals are broken and the entire record of judgments is executed. The seventh seal contains the seven trumpets, and the seventh trumpet contains the seven vials. In this sense the seventh seal reaches to the very end of the tribulation period.

(c) The *symbolism* of the seals and the horses must not be overlooked. The seals are the legal protection for the title deed through the centuries.

The title deed had long been made by a transaction between the Father and the Son, and the deed had been filed away until the appointed time. When the fullness of time was come, God sent forth His Son, who at Calvary paid the redemptive price with His own life's blood. Now He is fully qualified to open the seals and enter into the possession of His property. At this moment the time has come to take possession. The horses of judgment with their riders signify strength and power, and suggest the natural agents used of God to carry out His judgment (Job 39:19-25; II Kings 6:15-18; Zech. 1:8-10; 6:1-8).

(d) The *significance* of the opening of these seals and the events following therefrom may be described as providential judgments. Christ is not appearing immediately in the earth to execute judgment, as He will do when He returns in glory (19:11-21). In these judgments, He is allowing the world of sinful man to take its own course, which will lead to its own undoing. The spiritual state of the world following the rapture of the Church leads from one woe to another until finally cosmological disturbance runs its course throughout the entire fabric of nature, announcing to men that God is about to enter into the affairs of men and bring immediate judgment.

(e) The *seventieth week of Daniel* (Dan. 9:24-27), yet unfulfilled, will begin with the rapture of the Church and the opening of the first seal. "Hereafter" of Revelation 4:1 is the time signal for the beginning of the opening of the seals. The catching away of the Church (I Thess. 4:16-17; II Thess. 2:6-7) ushers in the tribulation period. This week of years has particular relation to Israel and the working out of God's purpose among the nations. During this time the Lord will again deal with Israel and the nations as He did in Egypt. A particular cycle will run its course again. God has been dealing with the nations by invitation, explanation, exhortation, demonstration. But during this period He will resort to compulsion. His last argument will be force.

(f) The *similarity* of the seals with material recorded in Mark 13, Luke 21 and Matthew 24 is significant. Compare the white horse and rider with those coming in the name of Christ (Matt. 24:5); the red horse with the wars and rumors of wars (Matt. 24:6-7); the black horse with famines, pestilences and the like (Matt. 24:7); the pale horse with the things that naturally follow upon the above (Matt. 24:6-7); the souls under the altar with the persecution mentioned (Matt. 24:9-22); the cosmological disturbances with those listed in Christ's account (Matt. 24:7, 29); and the seventh seal, including the trumpets and vials, with the account in Matthew 24:30-31).

2. Exposition.

(a) The *first seal*, the judgment of strong delusion (vv. 1-2). The Lamb is the ultimate origin of this judgment, for He is the one who opens the seal. It is the living creature who is the mediate origin, for he is the one who commands the horse and rider to "go." The American Standard Version eliminates the words "and see," and correctly so. And the word "come" in the original is as correctly translated "go." In this place, it makes better sense if the command to the horse and rider is "go." The appearance of the horse as white makes one think of the white horse in Revelation 19:11 and following. But this one cannot be Christ, for Christ is the one who holds the little book in His hands and tears away the seal. Without a doubt this is the one who comes in the name of Christ (Matt. 24:5) and is masquerading as the Christ. This is the judgment of strong delusion that God will send on men during the tribulation because they have rejected the Christ. This is the Antichrist (II Thess. 2:3-12). The bow, which is a long-range weapon of war, suggests that this is a providential judgment. The crown represents the rise of Antichrist to power (Rev. 13:2-4), and the fact that he comes "conquering and to conquer" marks the progressive career of the man, adding one triumph after another until he reaches the apex of his career (Dan. 7:24; Rev. 17:12-13). Since many interpreters of this book so easily mistake this personage for the Christ, it will not be surprising for the millions to be deluded by Antichrist.

(b) The *second seal,* the judgment of military might (vv. 3-4). The red horse clearly speaks of war that follows in the wake of the Antichrist. The devil is the god of war (Rev. 20:7-8; 12:7; 16:13-14) and Antichrist is a great military leader (Rev. 3:3-4), so it is perfectly logical that the red horse follows the white one. While the Antichrist may ingratiate himself with men at the outset by promising peace, it will not be long until he demonstrates that at heart he is a wild beast, and military force will be produced to compel subordination to his will. Peace will then be taken from the earth, and the "great sword" will be brandished so that universal strife will cover the earth. Gradually the true identity of the Antichrist will be manifest to the saints of God.

(c) The *third seal*, the judgment of physical deprivation (vv. 5-6). The black horse now rides forth picturing the famine and starvation that will follow closely upon the heels of war (Jer. 1:2-6; 14:1-2; Lam. 4:8-9; 5:10; Ezek. 4:10, 16-17). The balances suggest that a system of rationing will be enforced (Rev. 13:16-17). This means that there will be restriction of the food supply because of scarcity. This will be necessary because men and money will have been conscripted for military might. In order to keep the war machines rolling, the food will have been placed on a priority listing for the armies. Private citizens will be rationed and prices will soar. The penny is a day's wages and buys only enough for one person (Matt. 20:2, 9). Three measures of barley is the ration for animals, suggesting that people have finally been forced to the extreme by hunger. The command to hurt not the oil and wine, which is rich man's food, intimates that discrimination now takes place. Grains may cease because of war and devastation, but vines and trees, a hardier vegetation, not needing so much care, go on living and producing, and rich men alone are able to buy that food because of soaring prices.

(d) The *fourth seal*, the judgment of wholesale death (vv. 7-8). The word "pale" means green-like, as a corpse. The same word is used in Revelation 8:7, where it is translated "green grass." This pale horse is clearly named "Death" and "Hades" (ASV). It follows logically upon what precedes. War and famine, pestilence and wild beasts, bring death, and Hades swallows up the souls of those who die. During times of war, food shortage, famine, and pestilence, disease multiplies and wild beasts increase and grow ferocious. The colossal dimensions of war so far exceed anything known in human history that the toll in human lives is dreadful. One-fourth of the population finally succumbs to death as a result of war and its related causes. The destructiveness of war, the deprivation of famine, the devastation of disease and pestilence, and the ferocity of wild beasts turn the mountains and the plains into one vast graveyard.

(e) The *fifth seal*, the judgment of religious persecution (vv. 9-11). As the opening words here indicate, Christ is still opening the seals. Obviously the souls under the altar are the result of persecution carried on against the saints (Rev. 12:11; 13:7, 15). Their position under the altar is symbolism for the fact that these people have been purchased by the blood of Christ. They cry out, wondering how long it will be until judgment is inflicted on their persecutors. Their garments may indicate some sort of intermediate body. At least they are conscious and have some knowledge of things going on in the earth. They are informed that persecution will go on till the end and many more will join the ranks of the slain. This too is a logical sequel to the appearance of the Antichrist. Since the Church was caught out at the Rapture, it therefore follows that others will be saved who will belong to another company of saints. It is also implied that these people die because they come to Christ and repudiate the Antichrist. This he will not tolerate, so almost immediately the great persecution begins, and millions, having overcome the Antichrist by the blood of the Lamb and the word of their testimony, loved not their lives unto the death (Rev. 12:11).

(f) The *sixth seal,* the judgment of natural disturbance (vv. 12-17). Christ opens the seal and universal disturbance runs its course through heaven and earth. Without a doubt these are literal happenings, although described sometimes in the language of appearance. The result upon men is amazing, indicating that men everywhere carry within them a natural premonition of approaching judgment. Their prayers to avert wrath give the lie to those men today who claim to be atheists. These men recognize divine intervention. The testimony of the martyrs may explain how they know the director of these demonstrations, the Lamb. But these unusual demonstrations in nature indicate to men that delay in judgment is over and there is no one who will be able to withstand the execution of God's wrath. In the event that these cries for help are not to be interpreted as directed to a transcendent and supernatural God, then it is still true that men become suddenly conscious of a person and power that rises above the pantheistic god whom they have been worshiping. In vain do they cry out for the rocks and the mountains to cover them from the face of Him who sits upon the throne.

II. THE SAVING OF TWO MULTITUDES (chap. 7)

The opening of the sixth seal brings men to the recognition that God is sitting in judgment upon the earth. Up to this point judgment has been providential through the movements of men. But this seal is the announcement that the day of immediate judgment is at hand, and the seventh seal is the actual beginning of the day. Between these two seals, dispensing of judgment is arrested long enough to reveal grace operating in the midst of judgment. While no saved person can come into judgment, God can save men in the midst of judgment. The events of this parenthetical inset reach back to the beginning of the tribulation period, and forward to the very close of it. During this period God demonstrates how He saves two great throngs and the results which follow.

1. The sealed servants (vv. 1-8). The 144,000 point to God's discrimination in the midst of judgment.

(a) The *judgment* (v. 1) is pictured in the hands of four angels at the four corners of the earth, holding the four winds. These winds are for the purpose of spreading destruction on the earth, sea, and trees. The repetition of the number "four" suggests the universality of this judgment that is to take place under the seventh seal.

(b) The *sealing* (vv. 2-3) takes place during the interval between the sixth and seventh seal. This falls within the first three and one-half years of the tribulation period. It is limited to the servants of God, which suggests a spiritual relationship. From the outset of the tribulation period, the ministry of two witnesses (Rev. 11:3-7) is in progress. This is especially directed toward the people of Israel, though it is not necessarily confined to Israel. The result is that there is a turning to God among the Jews. Every Jew who turns to God turns away from the Antichrist. This disturbs the Antichrist, for he has made a treaty with the Jews for the space of seven years (Dan. 9:27). As this grows in proportion and spreads to the Gentiles he is forced to unloose persecution against the saints. In addition God is about to pour His wrath in ever-increasing force upon the wicked. To save some alive for the kingdom and for further ministry, 144,000 of the saved Jews are sealed to protect them from the physical judgments upon the world and from the wrath of the Antichrist. The seal indicates ownership, and reference to the forehead suggests that it is public. It is also implied that this seal will protect them physically from the coming judgments.

(c) The *identity* (vv. 4-8) of this group is clear. It is made up of 12,000 from each of the twelve tribes of the children of Israel. The tribe of Manasseh substitutes for Dan. It is difficult to explain why Ephraim is also left out. But Genesis 49:17 and Judges 18:30 may explain the exclusion of Dan. The old rabbis said that Genesis 49:17 was proof that Antichrist would arise out of that tribe. Almost any conclusion is pure speculation. This is one point we must leave to the Lord for revelation in the future. But the absence of these names is not to be supposed to suggest that Dan and Ephraim as tribes will not experience the blessing of the Lord in the Millennium, for their names so appear in the partition of the land as recorded in the last few chapters of Ezekiel (chaps. 40–48).

(d) The *purpose* of this sealing is not too clear. But it looks as though the 144,000 may be the first fruits "unto God and the Lamb" for the kingdom (Rev. 14:4), the result of the unusual ministry of the two witnesses during the first half of the tribulation period (11:1-8). Besides being protected in the midst of judgment, they may be saved for a ministry of preaching during the last half of the tribulation as suggested by a comparison of 14:1-5 with verse 6. Their ministry will bring about the salvation of the multitude described in verses 9-17 of this chapter. A more remote purpose may be to insure a remnant being ready to enter the millennial kingdom at the close of the tribulation.

2. The saved saints (vv. 9-17). During the period of greatest pers
by Antichrist, God saves this unnumbered multitude.

(a) *Description* (vv. 9-10). Here is a host from every nation, pe
Israel included, that cannot be numbered. Their white robes indicate that
they have been saved (v. 14), and also that they have suffered martyrdom
(cf. fifth seal). They are now in heaven before the rainbow-circled throne.
This does not mean all who are saved die during the period, for some must
enter the Millennium to populate the kingdom (Matt. 25:31-46).

(b) *Adoration* (vv. 11-12). They join with the hosts of heaven in worshiping God. Even though they had to pay the great price of death for
their testimony, salvation as a result of God's grace and power is more
than worth it.

(c) *Origination* (vv. 13-14). To John's question concerning their origin,
one of the elders gives the answer, "These are they which came out of
great tribulation." "The tribulation the great one" is the literal translation
of this in the original Greek. It makes this period a specific time: namely,
the last three and one-half years when Antichrist will turn all of his hatred
against the people of God, Jews and Gentiles alike (Jer. 30:7; Dan. 12:1;
Matt. 24:21-22).

(d) *Compensation* (vv. 15-17). Every spiritual blessing of presence with
the Lamb, the privilege to serve Him, the protection He gives and the
blessings He bestows, is their reward.

5

The Seventh Seal
and the Six Trumpets

Revelation 8 and 9

THE CHAPTER OUTLINED:

    I. The Seventh Seal and the Vision (8:15)
       1. The opening of the seventh and final seal
       2. The seven angels
       3. The smoking incense
       4. The fire from the altar

    II. The First Four Trumpet Judgments (8:6-13)
       1. The first trumpet
       2. The second trumpet
       3. The third trumpet
       4. The fourth trumpet
       5. The intermission

    III. The Fifth Trumpet Judgment (9:1-11)
       1. The origination
       2. The intention
       3. The description

    IV. The Sixth Trumpet Judgment (9:12-21)
       1. The origination
       2. The description
       3. The explanation

The seventh seal is the beginning of the day of God's wrath upon a wicked and rebellious humanity. During this period there will be increasing intensity in the judgments, and the judgments will gradually change from providential to the immediate intervention of God in human affairs. Since the first five verses of chapter 8 constitute a sort of introductory vision of the trumpet judgments, it will be in order to give some attention to this portion before proceeding with the trumpet judgments.

I. THE SEVENTH SEAL AND THE VISION (8:15)

1. The opening of the seventh and final seal is followed by an amazing response (v. 1). The immediate effects are felt in heaven. An ominous hush falls upon all the inhabitants of the celestial realm as they witness this event.

(a) The *cause* of this silence is the complete unrolling of the title deed to the universe. Under the seventh seal is the remainder of the divine operations for taking over the earth and expelling the usurpers. Judgments up to this point have been fearful in character, especially those loosed under the sixth seal. So ominous were they, that mankind universally is anticipating the day of wrath (6:15-17). And then, one of the angels of heaven, so much aware of the destruction to follow, even delays the opening of the seventh seal until the work of preservation on an elect company has been performed (9:4). Now the final seal has been torn away, and the unveiling of the remaining contents of the little book has been performed. It is of such character that all heaven is hushed into silence.

(b) The *character* of this silence may be described as the calm before the storm. Silence marks the climax of events and is sometimes far more eloquent than noise. The storm of judgment is about to break upon the world of wicked men and women. It is so devastating in character that silence greets it in heaven. No response could more adequately declare the terror that lies ahead than this awe-inspired silence.

(c) The *company* compelled to silence is made up of the inhabitants of heaven. The previous glimpse into heaven reveals the fact that this company consists of angels, living creatures, and the elders. Moments before they were engaged in tumultous adoration and praise of the One who sits on the throne and of the Lamb. But now the Lamb has opened the seventh seal, and all this joyful acclamation is suddenly silenced, so effectively silenced that for the space of one half hour, almost an eternity to those gathered about the throne, not a sound escapes them. The calamities they are about to witness are so awful that even a holy company rejoicing in the triumphs of the triune God can no longer continue their rejoicing over the defeat of the enemy. This fact alone ought to hush the hearts of men into careful consideration of what it will mean to go through this time of woe upon the earth. If heaven gasps in horror at the prospect, then men ought to rush headlong into the arms of Jesus for protection.

2. **The seven angels** to whom were given the seven trumpets now come into view (v. 2). Notice carefully the fact that the seven trumpets are a part of the seventh seal, and are not to be construed as another review of the judgments under the six seals.

(a) The *seven angels* are apparently a select group, for the definite article "the" is used of them. However, they are not to be confused with the seven angels holding the vials of wrath (15:1). Gabriel may be one of them, though no one can assert this definitely.

(b) These angels *stand before God,* or in God's presence. The same thing is declared by Gabriel of himself (Luke 1:19). The meaning of this fact can be understood by reading Esther 1:14. This certainly marks the place of power, dignity, and service (Heb. 1:7, 14).

(c) *Seven trumpets* are given to these angels. This denotes a sovereign action, and the judgments which follow are not providential. In fact, there is a gradual change in character and severity from the seals to the vials. The seals are for the most part providential in character and relatively severe. The trumpets are semi-providential and increasingly severe. The vials are immediate judgments from God and very severe.

The symbolism of the trumpets may not at first appear. It is therefore in point to ask the question concerning its significance. The trumpet is not an instrument placed in the hands of the angels and upon which they blow a blast. This is clearly revealed in the words describing the action of the seventh angel (Rev. 10:7). It reads: "But in the days of the voice of the seventh angel, when he shall begin to sound." The word translated "sound" is the word for trumpet. Thus it becomes clear that it is the voice of the angel that is placed under the figure of a trumpet. The angelic voice in its strength and power exceeds the ordinary voice as the blast of a trumpet exceeds ordinary sound.

3. **The smoking incense** and the prayers of the saints are encouragements to God's people (vv. 3-4). There is an angel-priest officiating at the altar. Some think this is Christ. But this is not necessary. The altar is in the court of the tabernacle. It is the altar of burnt offering. From this altar the golden censer was used to carry the fire to the golden altar of incense in the holy place. The angel receives incense, which is symbolical of the sweet

savor of Christ (Eph. 5:2), and this is offered up along with the prayers of all the saints to God upon the golden altar of incense. The ascent of both of these to God is pleasing to Him, the sweet savor of Christ satisfying Him in the behalf of all those who have accepted Christ (Eph. 5:2), and the prayers of all the saints calling for the fulfillment of all His promises to bring in the kingdom (Rev. 5:8).

4. The fire from the altar is symbolic of judgment being done in the earth (v. 5). The same instrument that offers up the incense is used to pour out judgment upon men. From the same altar that salvation comes, so also does judgment come upon wicked men (II Cor. 2:15; 10:28-29). The same fire that demanded the death of Christ in order to secure the salvation of men will destroy men who reject Christ (Heb. 12:29). When the fire is cast into the earth, voices, thunderings, and lightnings follow. These are indicative of the law of God in judgment upon men who have broken the law and rejected the only deliverance, namely, Christ (Exod. 19:12-20; 20:18-19; Rev. 4:5).

II. THE FIRST FOUR TRUMPET JUDGMENTS (8:6-13)

Heaven itself is now ready to execute judgment upon the wicked world as set forth in the first five verses of this chapter; the angels now prepare to inflict the penalty (v. 6).

1. The first trumpet (v. 7). The language of this verse is that of appearance, but it depicts actualities and not mere symbols of something else. Indeed it is picturesque. The judgment consists of hail, fire, and blood, which means hail and lightning with a blood-red color. The objects of judgment are the earth, especially trees and vegetation on a worldwide scale. The third part of trees and all grass are burned up. Compare this with Exodus 9:23-28. The purpose of this judgment, like the plagues of Egypt, is to teach men that those things upon which they have depended as the primary source of life, health, and happiness are after all dependent upon a supernatural creator and sustainer. The very fact that this lesson is necessary indicates that the world of men will at last have reverted back to the paganism of the past. They will have become pantheistic in their explanation of the universe, denying the existence of a God who is transcendent, before, above, outside, and separate from His creation, and identifying God with the creation. This, then, becomes the purpose of God in the first three trumpet judgments.

2. The second trumpet (vv. 8-9). The language follows the same pattern as in the description of the first trumpet. Here we read of a great mountain burning with fire. This may refer to a meteoric mass from the sky falling headlong into the sea, perhaps the Mediterranean Sea. The result is to turn a third part of the sea a blood-red color and bring about the death of a third part of the life in the sea. Death may be caused by the chemical reaction in the water, such as radioactivity following atomic explosion. The third part of ships may be destroyed by the violence of the waters produced by the falling of the mass.

3. The third trumpet (vv. 10-11). The descriptive language is still that of appearance. This time we see a great star, perhaps a meteor, definitely producing some chemical reaction in the waters into which it falls. It may have broken up when it hit the earth's atmosphere and become like dust. It would then spread out over a wide area. It is poisonous, but not always fatal. In the Greek the name "Wormwood" is "Absinthe." In some places men use this to make an aromatic cocktail which produces a dead drunk. Now God gives men their fill. The third part of rivers and fountains of water are struck, resulting in the death of many (Jer. 9:13-15).

4. The fourth trumpet (v. 12). Continuing with the same sort of language, this verse describes a reduction of light both as to amount and as to time. From the sun, moon, and stars the quantity of light is reduced by one third, and the length of time these shine is reduced by one third (Isa. 13:9-10). The earth is only affected indirectly. But the purpose of the judgment is primarily to teach men that these luminaries are not gods but the creations of God. When the ten plagues were brought upon Egypt, the purpose was to teach the Egyptians that the things they worshiped were not gods in any sense of the word, and that the Jehovah whom the Israelites worshiped and they despised was the real God. Here the same thing is true.

5. The intermission (v. 13). An eagle (ASV) is now seen flying through the midst of the heaven. Do not associate this with Matthew 24:28. Vultures gather about dead carrion, not eagles. The eagle is heard to cry with a loud voice, "Woe, woe, woe, to the inhabiters of the earth." If God made an ass to speak, surely He could cause an eagle to do likewise. Since the eagle is a symbol of judgment, that is precisely the nature of his message. The three remaining trumpets are so dreadful as to be called woes (Deut. 28:49; Jer. 48:40). Let those who read therefore be especially intent upon the learning the nature of these woes. The information should be a warning.

III. THE FIFTH TRUMPET JUDGMENT (9:1-11)

1. The origination of the locusts (vv. 1-3).

(a) The *star* (v. 1). When this star is seen, it is not in the process of falling, but has already fallen (ASV). It is not a natural star, as the pronouns and actions indicate. Since we have already learned that stars are symbols for angels (1:20), it may be concluded that this is an angel. This one is apparently in charge of the pit (20:1-3). But this angel is not Satan, for Satan torments the righteous and not the wicked, as these locusts turn out to do (vv. 4-5; 12:17). If the word "fallen" is taken in the moral sense, this may suggest that he is forced to obey God.

(b) The *abyss* (vv. 1-2). The King James Version reads "bottomless pit," whereas the American Standard Version is more correct, reading "pit of the abyss." But the Greek is even better, "well of the abyss," a place much lower, perhaps, than the very lowest part of the abyss itself. It is very possible that this is the place where the wicked spirits are confined, and may be the same as lower Sheol or lower Hades, or Tartarus (II Peter 2:4). Satan will be confined to the abyss for one thousand years (Rev. 20:1-3), and demons are also tormented in this place (Luke 8:27-31, "deep"). It most certainly is the place of the dead as indicated by the reference to Christ in Romans 10:7 (Greek), though Christ did not go to the lowest part of the abyss.

(c) The *smoke* (v. 3). The smoke came out of the place called the well of the pit (v. 2). It was a great smoke that darkened the sun and air and was as the smoke of a great furnace. The smoke was not the locusts, for the locusts came out of the smoke (v. 3). The smoke doubtless has reference to the torment these creatures suffer. In other places we read of the smoke of their torment (14:11; cf. also Luke 8:27-31). The furnace refers to the place of torment where judgment is being meted out (Rev. 18:9-10, 15, 18; 19:3; 20:10; II Peter 2:4; Jude 6-7).

(d) The *locusts* (v. 3). The locusts come out of the smoke with power to torture men like scorpions.

2. The intention of the locusts (vv. 4-6).

(a) The *realm* of their power is unsaved men (v. 4). They must not hurt trees, grass, or green things. They dare not hurt men with the seal in their foreheads. But they may hurt men who do not possess the seal.

(b) The *extent* of their power is limited to five months (v. 5). Their force can go only so far. They dare not kill, but they may sting like the scorpion.

(c) The *result* of this exercise of force is tremendous (v. 6). The torment produces such excruciating pain that men seek death and are not able to bring it about. Though they desire to die, death always eludes them. The reason death eludes them is to teach them that God is the one who holds the soul in life. Not until He is ready to release the spirit will death come. God has His own times and seasons for every person. In the case of these people He preserves life even through great suffering in order to teach them a lesson. This lesson will become more evident a bit later.

3. The description of the locusts (vv. 7-11).

(a) The *shapes* of these creatures are hideous (v. 7). They are like horses prepared for battle. Crowns of gold seem to be upon their heads. Their faces are like men, their hair like women, their teeth like lions. They have on breastplates as of iron. And their tails were like those of a scorpion.

(b) The *sound* of their wings was like that of many chariots in the rush toward battle (v. 9).

(c) Their *stings* were in their tails, and with these they tormented men (v. 10).

(d) The *sovereign* over them was the angel of the bottomless pit whose name in Hebrew means "destruction," and in Greek means "destroyer" (v. 11).

(e) This *species* of locusts is not the ordinary kind, as indicated by the place from which they come, the things they do not eat, their shapes and description, and their purpose. Moreover, ordinary locusts do not have a king (Prov. 30:27; Exod. 10:14). The explanation of them will be delayed until we come to verses 20 and 21.

IV. THE SIXTH TRUMPET JUDGMENT (9:12-21)

Verse 12 is descriptive of the judgment that is just past and the one that is to come. Both are woes.

1. The origination of the infernal horsemen (vv. 12-15).

(a) The *ultimate* source of this judgment is the voice from the horns of the golden altar (v. 13). This voice is in response to the prayers of the saints and is based upon the efficacy of the work of Christ. The horns signify power to answer. The same voice that was intended to call for mercy, instead calls for judgment.

(b) The *mediate* source of the judgment is the sixth angel (v. 14). This angel is to loose the four angels bound in the great river Euphrates, where evil began on earth (Zech. 5:8-11), where false religion began (Gen. 4:3; 10:9-10; 11:4), and where it will come to its end (Rev. 17–18).

(c) The *immediate* source of judgment is the four angels and their army (vv. 15-16). These angels are limited to a certain time, namely, 13 months, during which they are allowed to slay only a third part of men. This they do with the amazing army at their command. This means that more than half the population of the world has now suffered death. As a result of the opening of the fourth seal one-fourth of the population suffered death. Now a third of that which is left suffers death. From other sources death results: persecution, destruction in the sea, and wormwood. This means that more than half the population of the earth has perished within just a few years, perhaps three. Using the population figure of the world today, this would mean that more than one billion 500 million would have died.

2. The description of the army (vv. 16-19). For size this army is 200 million. And while it is possible that this may refer to men and machines, it seems very unlikely. The appearance of these horsemen is terrifying (v. 17). They have breastplates of fire and jacinth and brimstone. This probably is again the language of appearance. The heads of the horses are like the heads of lions. And out of their mouths issue fire and smoke and brimstone, by which a third part of men are killed. Their power is in their mouths, but also in their tails, which tails are like serpents and have heads with which they can hurt men. While a third part of men die, many other men simply suffer torment from these creatures.

It is a temptation at this point to yield to the desire to interpret these horsemen in terms of modern warfare. Tanks, machine guns, flame throwers, and many other varieties of modern warfare so easily fit the imagery. Some insist that this is the army from the East, beyond the Euphrates, from China, Japan, India, marching toward the Battle of Armageddon two hundred million strong. This may be true in the light of Revelation 16:12-16. But it seems best to keep to the immediate context for the explanation, suggesting that this may throw further light on another aspect of the passage in chapter 16.

3. The explanation for the fifth and sixth trumpets (vv. 20-21).

(a) *"These plagues"* of verse 20 refer back to the fifth and sixth trumpets. These woes are a more dreadful kind than in the earlier trumpets (8:13; 9:12), and result in the death of many and the torment of many more.

(b) The *response* of the living to them explains them. The living continue to worship what they have worshiped: namely, the works of their hands which are images, and demons (Greek) who are represented by the images (I Cor. 8:4-5; 10:20). All Gentile pagan worship was and is demonic and will be in the end time. As a judgment upon men God gives them their own gods.

(c) The *incorrigibility* of sinners is marked by the fact that they are determined to continue on in sin, murders, sorceries, fornication, thefts, all of these associated with pagan idolatry and demon worship.

(d) Here we have the *fulfillment* of I Timothy 4:1-3 and II Thessalonians 2:9-12.

In the end time there will be an outbreak of demonic worship which may become well-nigh universal (I Tim. 4:1-3). Satan will sponsor this among those who have rejected the truth, and they will be led along by means of effective error (II Tim. 4:3-4; II Thess. 2:9-12). Since men have preferred to reject the truth in Christ, they will follow demons. And God will grant to them their own gods so that they may learn how utterly impure and malignant they are. This will settle the question about the goodness of the "isms." The response of men will clearly reveal that they have become confirmed in sin and are ripe for judgment, for they refuse to turn from their iniquity and continue to blaspheme God. Thus the grotesque locusts and the infernal horsemen seem to be swarms of demons from the pit.

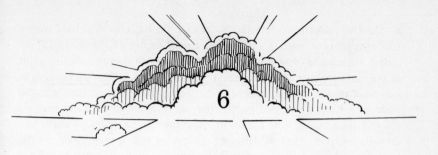

The Sun-Faced Angel
and the Seventh Trumpet

Revelation 10 and 11

THE CHAPTER OUTLINED:

I. The Sun-Faced Angel and Title Deed (Chap. 10)
1. The mighty angel
2. Now the mystery of God
3. The man's action

II. The 70th Week of Daniel and Israel (11:1-13)
1. The preparatory measuring
2. The two witnesses
3. Satanic war
4. The divine wonders

III. The Seventh Trumpet Judgment (11:14-19)
1. The divine announcement
2. The vocal proclamation
3. The great acclamation
4. The sacred ratification

The two chapters of Revelation forming the basis for this study constitute two literary insets for the most part. Chapter 11, verses 14-19, describes the effects from the blowing of the seventh trumpet. At this point in the narrative it is time to explain two things that will invariably arise in the mind of the careful student of Scripture. They were certainly in the mind of John as he viewed events from his place in heaven. First, how are matters proceeding with Christ in expelling the usurpers of earth and taking over possession of His own property; and second, how are the fortunes of Israel turning out as the judgments upon the earth increase in their intensity? The first problem is settled by the information of chapter 10. In this chapter answer is given to the mystery of God (10:7). The second problem is discussed in 11:1-13, producing awe and consternation in John. The climax is reached in heaven with the blowing of the seventh trumpet (11:14-15), and is followed immediately by the ferocious hostility that is produced among the nations (11:16-19).

I. THE SUN-FACED ANGEL AND TITLE DEED (chap. 10)

1. The mighty angel and the book (vv. 1-4). As the panorama of events passes before the eyes of John, his attention is drawn again to the little book he saw in the hands of the One upon the throne and which was finally taken by Christ. Then, one by one, the seven seals were removed. When John last viewed the book it was still in the hands of Christ, and He had just torn away the seventh seal (8:1). Now the book is in the hands of the mighty angel (10:2).

(a) The *identification* of this angel provides interesting information (v. 1). Many able expositors insist that it is Christ. But there does not seem to be any absolute reason why this must be true. The text here merely says "another" mighty angel. Certainly in the record of this revelation up to this point many mighty angels have been seen by the writer, all of them entrusted with some very important tasks. This is merely another, for God is not running short of angels to do His bidding. Christ sends this one from heaven with delegated authority to perform a great task for Him. Christ remains in heaven directing the movement of affairs from the throne and does not return to earth until 19:11-21; 10:4, 8. Since this angel is the direct representative of Christ, that is sufficient to explain why he must swear by God and Christ (v. 6).

(b) The *description* of this angel is the thing that leads some men to conclude that it is Christ. He is clothed with a cloud, which may be a cloud of glory. But this feature may be explained by the fact that he is representing Christ. The rainbow upon his head shows that his work of judgment is going to be tempered with mercy, in this way carrying out the purpose of the rainbow-circled throne (4:2-3). The fact that his face shines as the sun, even though so close to the statement about Christ (1:16), only indicates that his authority is supreme as the delegated agent of Christ. "Countenance" in 1:16 and "face" in 10:1 are different words in the original Greek. The feet of the angel, described in this verse as like pillars of fire, are set for the exercise of judgment.

(c) The *possessing* of property is the meaning of the actions of the angel (vv. 2-4). In his hands is the little book, the title deed to the universe. It is now completely open. Christ has removed every one of the seven seals, indicating that He is now ready to take possession of His property. For this purpose He sends a mighty angel to discharge this task. With the book in his hand, the angel places one foot upon the sea and the other upon the land. No more significant action could be performed by a person to signify the taking of possession of his own property (cf. Joshua 1:3). With a loud voice he cries as a lion, thus signifying that he will use force to hold and defend his possession. Then seven thunders utter their voices. If it were not for the fact that these thunders are sealed, one might search out their meaning. But here it would be useless. However, one thing is clear: thunder certainly gives one the general sense of judgment.

2. Now the mystery of God is announced (vv. 5-7). Here is something every saint of God through all the ages has wanted to know.

(a) The *guarantee* that the angel's message is true is in the act of swearing (vv. 5-6). His mission is so important that he lifts his hand and swears by Him who is greater than himself, by the creator of the universe. Swearing is the calling upon a higher person or power to witness to the veracity of a statement with the added incentive of punishment if the statement is not true. This is not to be confused with cursing, which is calling down evil upon the head of some one; or with blasphemy, which is affirmation of untruth about God or the things of God; or with profanity, which is making common the name of God without any purpose.

(b) The *substance* of the angel's message is concerned with the time for taking action in judgment (v. 6). The King James Version says "time no longer." But the sense is that no more time will pass before judgment is executed. The American Standard Version has cleared up this difficulty by translating the phrase "delay no longer" (cf. Matt. 24:40 and following). This is the statement guaranteed by the act of swearing on the part of the angel. This is the one item of information that has remained a mystery to the saints across the millenniums. It is the one thing that baffled John and with which he was confronted when he first saw the little book and no one was found to open it. Time will go on forever, but the time for the carrying out of an event in the plan of God will not be delayed any longer.

(c) The *mystery* of God is to be finished, a mystery which was revealed to the prophets of old as "good tidings" (v. 7, ASV). This finish comes when the seventh angel begins to sound. The beginning of the seventh trumpet (11:15) is in the middle of the tribulation period. Its effects run to the very conclusion of the tribulation period. In fact, the effects will be progressively realized over the period of the thousand-year reign and will reach their culmination when the last enemy is subdued (I Cor. 15:24-28).

(d) The *message* given to the prophets and taking the nature of "good tidings" is an answer to one of their greatest questions (v. 7). What they could not understand was why a God of holiness and power allowed evil to go unpunished and good people to suffer. Or, to put it another way, why does not God establish His righteous kingdom and rule over men (Hab. 1:2-4; Ps. 73)? When Christ came and was rejected, the mystery became deeper. Though the mysteries of the kingdom were set forth in seven parables (Matt. 13), the time for the clear revelation has just now arrived. There will be no longer delay in the execution of judgment upon wicked men. The proof that this is the general meaning is recorded in Revelation 11:15-17, immediately following the blowing of the seventh trumpet.

3. The man's action with the little book (vv. 8-11). The voice that has been speaking to John now speaks again, and it can be none other than Christ speaking from heaven (v. 1; cf. 1:10; 4:1; 10:4).

(a) At the *command* to take the book which is in the hand of the angel, John responds (vv. 8-9).

(b) By *reflection* upon the message which lies on the surface one effect is produced. By thorough digestion of its deeper meaning an adverse effect follows (v. 9; cf. Ezek. 3:1; Jer. 16:17-18).

(c) John *rejoices* over the message as it reaches his mouth. The first effect is just like honey in the mouth. Joy comes to him because judgment is to be executed upon the wicked in general who are the enemies of his people Israel (v. 10).

(d) But fuller *realization* of the meaning of the message brings bitterness in the belly. It fills his mind and heart with consternation and revulsion (v. 10). Judgment upon the wicked brings rejoicing, but the far-reaching effects of this judgment also include his own people Israel (chaps.

11–13). They will enter into great tribulation.

(e) *Responsibility,* however, to prophesy this very message is committed to John (v. 11). He must prophesy before many peoples, and nations, and tongues, and kings. This he has done in recording the message which follows.

II. THE 70th WEEK OF DANIEL AND ISRAEL (11:1-13)

From the standpoint of chronology this portion of the Word of God is most important. From the prophetic standpoint, it is indispensable to the understanding of the movement of events during the tribulation period. It is the revelation and explanation of Daniel's 70th Week.

1. The preparatory measuring of the temple (vv. 1-2). The angel of 10:1-2 is directing this operation.

(a) The *occasion* for this measuring is the angel's mission into the world to take possession of the property of the Lord (v. 1). It is the business of the angel to direct in the ejection of the usurpers so that the proper inhabitants can be settled in their possession. As a symbolic move he places a reed, a measuring stick, in the hands of John and orders him to measure the temple and the worshipers. This certainly points to the characteristic action of taking over possession (Ezek. 40:3; 45:1-7; Zech. 2:1-5).

(b) The *objects* which are being measured are definitely Jewish (vv. 1-2). The temple, the sacred place of worship, is to be measured. The altar is included. And the people who worship in this temple are also to be measured. This signifies that God is beginning again to deal with the nation Israel. This is definitely Daniel's "70th Week" (Dan. 9:27).

From the days of the Babylonian Captivity God has not been dealing with Israel as a nation. Foreigners have been in possession of the land, the temple area, the altar, and in control over the people of Israel. This was only intensified with the Roman destruction of Jerusalem and the further dispersion of Israel among the nations of the world. At the point where John stands in history, there is no visible hope for Israel. But the prophecies of the Old Testament still hold out hope (Hosea 3:4-5). And now John is ushered into a vision and a personal experience that confirms and renews the promises of the Old Testament. The measuring of the temple and altar and the nation means that God is going to take up His residence again in the midst of His people and reassemble them in the land of their fathers. The final week of years in the history of Israel as set forth in Daniel's prophecy of the 70 weeks is now about to be fulfilled. But things which involve Gentiles are not to be measured. For God is not dealing with Gentiles during this period, except in judgment, and the times of the Gentiles are running out (Luke 21:24).

(c) The *outcome* of this measuring is significant (v. 2). The return of the Jews to their land and the opening of the "70th Week" of Daniel is signalized by a covenant made with Antichrist (Dan. 9:27). This contract with Antichrist embraces a plan covering seven years of time. During the first three and one-half years the Jews enjoy great prosperity at his hands. Then in the midst of the week of seven years he breaks the covenant and begins persecution of them. This persecution extends over the last three and one-half years. It is here referred to as a period of 42 months. During this time the holy city and the temple are desecrated by Antichrist (II Thess. 2:3-4). The altar is no longer used, and sacrifice and oblation cease (Dan. 9:27). And God's people Israel suffer awful persecution at the hands of Antichrist (Rev. 12:6, 13; Dan. 12:1; Matt. 24:21).

2. The two witnesses and their testimony (vv. 3-6). It is possible that John does not see this, but that Christ merely tells him about it. In any event, they draw their own picture in vivid detail.

(a) The *interval* of their testimony is first given (v. 3). By comparing 12:6 with 11:2, you will note that the final three and one-half years of the tribulation period are under consideration. It may therefore be concluded that verse 3 points to the first half of the tribulation period. During this period Christ gives authority to His two witnesses to prophesy. This is referred to in Malachi 4:4-6, pointing back to the Law of Moses as the basis for the kingdom, and includes the gospel of grace as it relates to the kingdom (Rev. 14:6). This message will lead men to Christ and the experience of the new birth, which is the condition of entrance (John 3:3, 5). It is the ministry of these two witnesses and the response to it that incites the wrath of Antichrist and provides the occasion for breaking the covenant with the Jews (v. 7; cf. Dan. 9:27).

(b) The *importance* of their testimony cannot be overestimated (v. 4). They are the two olive trees and the two candlesticks or lamps that stand before the Lord (Zech. 4). They represent the Lord in royal and priestly rights here among men. Oil from these trees is a symbol of the Spirit, and in them it gives the light of the Spirit amidst the terrible darkness of this period. By their testimony, it is my opinion, they bring about the conversion of the 144,000 who will become the witnesses during the final half of the tribulation period.

(c) The *instruments* given to them for the purpose of carrying on their ministry are supernatural (vv. 5-6). For protection they are given a miraculous power to cause fire to proceed out of their mouth (v. 5). This may be simply the power to speak and bring death. For evidence of their divine authority, they can shut up heaven from raining, turn water into blood, and smite the earth. Without a doubt one of these witnesses is Elijah (Mal. 4:4-6; James 5:17-18; I Kings 17:1; 18:42; Matt. 11:13-15; John 1:21; Luke 1:15-17). Moses may be the other (Mal. 4:4; Matt. 17:4; II Peter 1:16; Exod. 7:20; 9:14). However, others think it may be Enoch (Jude 14-15). The Jews referred vaguely to another prophet (John 1:21-23). Moses and Elijah figured so prominently in the history of Israel that they could well be the human instruments in the hands of the Lord to bring about the amazing conversion and sealing of the 144,000. Moses was the great lawgiver in Israel who stood against a Gentile king of his time, while Elijah led the opposition against apostasy in the darkest day in the history of the northern kingdom of Israel.

3. **Satanic war** and the two witnesses (vv. 7-10). An amazing series of events now begins when Antichrist rises up against the witnesses.

(a) Their *destruction* takes place only after they have finished their testimony (v. 7). Once they have finished the task for which God sent them, the powers of protection are withdrawn and Antichrist is permitted to kill them. The war begins against the two witnesses, but it continues against the Jews for the next three and one-half years. The beast of this passage can be none other than Antichrist (Rev. 13:1; 17:3, 8; 19:19-20; 20:10).

(b) The *humiliation* of the two witnesses is the greatest ignominy the Beast can imagine (vv. 8-9). The dead bodies of these two men are allowed to remain in the streets of the city where all can see. The spiritual condition of the city is described by the words "Sodom" and "Egypt." In order to leave no confusion, it is declared that this is Jerusalem, but a Jerusalem under the domination of Antichrist.

The publicity of this event is far reaching. Not only are all in the city able to see these bodies for a period of three and one-half days, but perhaps peoples all over the world also see it through the medium of television. The descent and proper thing to do would be to give immediate burial, especially because of the hot climate. But leaving the bodies there to decay and decompose and produce stench only adds to the shame and satisfies more fully the insatiable hatred of the Beast against them. The interest of all mankind centers upon this event. This is to be explained by the fact that it has a definite relation to the king of the entire world. By this time the Antichrist has risen to absolute power. All other world powers have been subjugated in one way or another, until at last he has attained that place after which he has sought. Now the nations of mankind not only acclaim him as their king, but they also follow every event and circumstance of his career with intense interest. At this point the one event that is engaging the interest of the entire world is the hostility between the Beast and the two unusual witnesses for God. This now reaches climactic proportions.

(c) Then *exultation* breaks out among the people, as if the shame already experienced were not enough (v. 10). All the inhabitants of the earth, it appears, burst into rejoicing, and send tokens of their joy to one another. This cause is simply that these men proclaimed a message which tormented them, and also that a company of 144,000 Jews were saved and rebelled against Antichrist, which by then was regarded as a direct insult both to Antichrist and also to themselves, for they had pledged allegiance to him.

4. The divine wonders and their purpose (vv. 11-13). When it would appear that Antichrist and his followers have gained the victory, the most amazing things take place.

(a) The *resurrection* of these two witnesses takes place in the sight of many (v. 11). It is the Spirit of life, none other than the Holy Spirit, who raises them (Rom. 8:11). When they stand up before the very eyes of those who witnessed their death and the three and one-half days of shame, astonishment turns to great fear, for the apparent defeat of the witnesses is now turned into triumph.

(b) The *rapture* of these two saints into heaven adds to the amazement of the people (v. 12). A voice from heaven calls them up hither (Rev. 4:1), and in a cloud of glory they ascend into heaven before the eyes of a quaking multitude (I Thess. 4:17). By this, both their testimony and their character as righteous men are vindicated.

(c) *Retribution* is now visited upon the wicked city where they suffered shame (v. 13). The earthquake coming either simultaneous with or shortly following their ascension provides further proof for their character and testimony. The damage is a tenth part of the city with casualties of up to 7,000 men so moves the people to profound conviction and fright that they give glory to the God of heaven.

III. THE SEVENTH TRUMPET JUDGMENT (11:14-19)

1. The divine announcement of the final woe brings to the attention of the reader the fact that judgment is now moving into its final phase (v.

14). Each woe has been increasingly worse, and this one will bring complete victory to the Messiah.

2. The vocal proclamation of victory now realized follows the blowing of the seventh trumpet (v. 15). In heaven Christ has taken over the kingdom of this world, and it is now His. He will reign for ever and ever (ASV). It will only be a matter of time (three and one-half years) until all the usurpers are expelled and judged.

3. The great acclamation of praise comes from the elders (vv. 16-18). It begins with worship (v. 16), merges into thanksgiving (v. 17), and concludes with a rehearsal of the events yet to come (v. 18).

4. The sacred ratification proceeds from the heavenly temple, is based on the law, and shows that God keeps His covenants (v. 19). This will be an encouragement to John, for the Jews are about to enter tribulation.

The Sun-Clothed Woman
and the Dragon

Revelation 12

THE CHAPTER OUTLINED:

I. The Conflict of the Past (vv. 1-5)
   1. The woman
   2. The dragon
   3. The conflict

II. The Conflict in Heaven (vv. 7-12)
   1. The conflict
   2. The concern

III. The Conflict in the Future (vv. 6, 13-17)
   1. The battle of the land
   2. The battle of the wilderness
   3. The battle of the remnant

Revelation 12 is one of the most important chapters in the entire Bible as well as in the Book of Revelation. Once one comes to know its significance, the confusing issues of history and prophecy become plain. In literary construction, this chapter is an inset. The lines of truth in it reach backward through the centuries to the time of Abraham and forward to the end of the tribulation period.

Chronologically this chapter should appear at this point in the unfolding of events during the tribulation period. Chapter 11 clearly indicates the fact that the story has reached the middle of the tribulation period. The two witnesses finish their testimony of three and one-half years (11:3, 7) and then suffer death at the hands of Antichrist. This is accompanied by Antichrist's breaking of his covenant with the Jews (Dan. 9:27), the ushering in of the three and one-half years of great tribulation upon the Jews (Rev. 11:2), and the war against the saints during the last half of the tribulation period (13:7).

The nation of Israel now comes into prominence. All of chapter 11 makes this clear. Since the great prophetic portions of the Old Testament concerning Israel are yet unfulfilled, and since in this 20th century there is great mystery surrounding Israel as a nation, it seems only logical that somewhere in the Word of God there should be information concerning fulfillment of promise to Israel and unraveling of the mystery concerning this ancient people. This premonition is realized in chapter 12.

Let every student of this great chapter realize right here that the understanding of this chapter is the key to the understanding of many things. It is the key to correct interpretation of the Book of Revelation, of the Bible, and of history. In this chapter will be found the story of the conflict of the ages. This conflict is not one of mere abstractions, such as right and wrong or good and evil. This is a conflict of great personalities.

The conflict gathers about the sun-clothed woman and the dragon. But into the picture come God, a man-child, Michael, and the angels. The scope of time involved in this conflict is tremendous. The past aspects of this conflict are described. The future of this conflict is also narrated. The great present age of grace, the Church Age, is not in view. The reason for this will be seen later. For the sake of more careful treatment the chapter is being divided into three divisions: (1) the conflict of the woman with the dragon in the past (vv. 1-5); (2) the conflict of the woman with the dragon in the heavens (vv. 7-12); (3) the conflict of the woman with the dragon in the future (vv. 6, 13-17).

I. THE CONFLICT IN THE PAST (vv. 1-5)

In these verses three main things are discussed: the woman, the dragon, and the conflict.

1. The woman (vv. 1-2). By careful examination of the Scriptures it will be found that a woman is used as a symbol of religion, false or true. Four such women appear in the Bible. Jezebel represents paganism and idolatrous worship (Rev. 2:20; I Kings 16:31). The scarlet woman represents false religion in general (Rev. 17). The bride of Christ represents the true church (Rev. 19). And the sun-clothed woman represents Judaism and the nation Israel (Rev. 12).

(a) The *appearance* of this woman clearly indicates her identity. She can be none other than Israel. She is clothed with the sun. The moon is under her feet. And the stars, twelve of them, make up the crown upon her head. There is only one place in the Bible where similar imagery is used of anyone, and that appears in the description of a dream which Joseph had and which he related to his father Jacob. Both Joseph and Jacob recognized the meaning of this dream (Gen. 37:9-11). It referred to the nation of Israel, which then was just beginning and was limited to the immediate family of Jacob.

(b) The *activity* of the woman from the time of Abraham to the birth of Christ is described in verse 2. The present tense of the verbs in this verse provide a dramatic setting. The woman is continuously with child. She is continually crying. She is continuously in the pain of travail. She is continuously experiencing labor to be delivered. She is continuously endeavoring to give birth to a child. Herein, then, are pictured the experiences of Israel as a nation from the moment she was brought into existence with the call of Abraham until the day Christ was born in Bethlehem. The entire message of the Old Testament from Genesis to Malachi describes what is here set forth in one verse.

(c) The *arrival* of the man-child is described in verse 5. The clearest possible interpretation, and the easiest, identifies this child with Christ. Prophetic Scripture promised that Christ would be born in Israel (Isa. 7:14; 9:6-7; Micah 5:2-3). And this anointed one to appear in Israel was to be God's Son who would rule the nations with a rod of iron (Isa. 9:6-7; Ps. 2:6-9). This woman cannot be the church. Any sensible interpretation of the Bible and history will not justify the position that this woman is the church. And surely the subsequent experience of the woman through three and one-half years of tribulation seals the fact that this woman is Israel (12:6).

(d) The *meaning* of the woman is marked by the word "wonder" (AV) or "sign" (RV) (v. 1). This word refers to something that has an inherent relation to the thing it signifies. In some sense of the word, it becomes evident what the Lord meant when he said to the Samaritan, "Salvation is of the Jews" (John 4:22). When the plan of salvation was devised in heaven, it was arranged that Christ should be united to humanity through the Jews. "For verily he took not on him the nature of angels; but he took on him the seed of Abraham" (Heb. 2:16).

2. The dragon (vv. 3-4). There is absolutely no doubt about the identity of this creature. Nevertheless the description is important.

(a) The *appearance* of the dragon is one that captures attention immediately (vv. 3, 9). The general appearance is that of a dragon, or monster, breathtaking and formidable. In size he is great, with tremendous proportions, suggesting his power and activity. He has a fiery color, or a brilliance like fire, betokening attractiveness rather than repulsiveness. The seven heads, the ten horns, and the crowns will be appearing again in chapters 13 and 17. The heads are mountains or governments energized by this monster (Rev. 17:9), and the ten horns are ten kings of the end time (Rev. 17:12). This monster is Satan (12:9), and his special representative, the Antichrist, is described in the same way (13:1).

(b) The *activity* of the dragon is described by the word "drew" of verse 4. It is a present tense and therefore sets forth the working of Satan through all the centuries of the past, present, and future up to his confinement in the bottomless pit. The stars are quite evidently angels, as verse 7 indicates. One-third of the angelic hosts joined with Satan in the insurrection in heaven sometime after creation. So completely successful was he in leading this rebellion in heaven that these angels continue to follow him to the very end of his career, at last to suffer everlasting destruction with him in the lake of fire (Matt. 25:41).

(c) The *attitude* of the dragon is set forth in the words, "And he did cast them to the earth" (v. 4). The word "cast" is used of a leader who causes others to follow him (cf. John 10:4). This particular statement is written by John as he stands at the very end and looks back over the career of Satan. From the moment Satan's heart was lifted up he has not changed. He set his heart on supplanting God and taking over the rule of the universe, and he presses toward the goal, no matter what it may mean to those who follow him. The result is that the angels who followed have suffered one judgment after another through the millenniums. They were cast out of the holy of holies in heaven, out of the holy mountain of God, out of the precincts of God's heaven into the aerial and stellar regions, and one day they will be cast out into the earth (v. 9). Some have already been cast into Tartarus (II Peter 2:4), and in God's time all who followed Satan will be cast into the lake of fire (Matt. 25:41).

(d) The *meaning* of the dragon is designated by the word "wonder" (v. 3). Through the centuries he has been masquerading as an angel of light (II Cor. 11:14). But now at last the great enemy of God and the archfiend of the universe is revealed in his true colors. What he was by nature was never known, but now he becomes clearly manifest.

3. The conflict (vv. 4-5). In graphic description the conflict between the nation Israel and Satan is now set forth.

(a) The *place* of the conflict is described as being "before the woman" (v. 4). Quite literally this reads, "in the eyes of the woman." Satan planted himself there when Israel was young and has continued there through the centuries. The woman could always see this ugly monster before her, though she may not have been able to identify him. He was ever present in the hostile nations of this world, over which he exercised control (Luke 4:6).

(b) The *period* of conflict is marked by the word "stood" (v. 4). In the American Standard Version the word is rendered "standeth," and it could well be translated "was standing." This covers the centuries from the moment of Israel's existence as a nation to the birth of Christ. And even after the child was born and caught up to heaven, the dragon has not ceased to hate and persecute the nation of Israel (v. 6). If the history of Israel is studied with this in mind, it becomes the most dramatic and breathtaking story in the annals of men. Review those incidents in the life of Abraham when his own life hung in the balance; this was also repeated in the lives of Isaac, Jacob, and the family of Jacob in Egypt. Think of the nation of Israel under Egyptian taskmasters, the precarious events in the flight from Egypt, the enemies encountered in the wilderness, those soul-stirring and perilous events during the conquest of the Promised Land, the times of stress within the kingdom when wicked men sought the life of the royal seed and it hung by a mere thread. Think of the Assyrian and Babylonian captivities, and that fateful night when the life of the whole nation was in the hands of a treacherous Haman. All these incidents and many more constituted the carefully planned conspiracy of Satan to destroy the woman Israel and do away with the promised Christ, the heir apparent to the throne.

(c) The *purpose* of this conflict is "to devour her child as soon as it was born" (v. 4). Satan was always aware that Israel was about to give birth to the Christ, who was the only threat to his unholy ambitions. Having set his eye upon the crown, he did not propose to let any contender stand in his way. If he could prevent the entrance of Christ into the world, or destroy Him after His entrance, nothing would then stand in his way to becoming the Lord of the universe. At Bethlehem, in the wilderness, at Nazareth, numbers of times during Jesus' ministry, and at last at the cross, Satan attempted to devour the Christ-child. But at the very moment he thought he had succeeded, he looked again only to see he had failed. The massacre of the babes of Bethlehem was his scheme. To escape being caught in this massacre, the Lord warned Joseph in a dream and he fled to Egypt. Even the return to Nazareth had to be delayed until the death of King Herod. Since the record is silent, no one knows how many times during the first thirty years of Christ's life some attempt was made by Satan to bring Him to an untimely end. During His public ministry this was experienced on more than one occasion. Satan sought to destroy Him in the wilderness of temptation, at His appearance in the synagogue in Nazareth, at the time of the second Passover. At the time of the third Passover it became dangerous for Christ to venture into Judea or the city of Jerusalem. One last desperate effort was made at the time of the fourth Passover. One from the inner circle betrayed Him into the hands of His enemies, and contrary to every law of God and man He was placed upon the cross. What Satan did not know was that Christ's "hour was come," and this death spelled out the defeat of Satan. But this wisdom "none of the princes of this world knew: for had they known it, they would not have crucified the Lord of glory" (I Cor. 2:8).

(d) The *rapture* of the man-child into heaven thwarted Satan in his evil intentions (v. 5). The "child was caught up unto God, and to his throne." The cross and the tomb were not all. The resurrection followed as unquestionable proof that Satan had miscalculated. Forty days more and Christ was raptured into the presence of God and to the position of power upon the throne (Eph. 1:20-22; Heb. 2:9), "from henceforth expecting till his enemies be made his footstool" (Heb. 10:13; cf. Ps. 110:1).

Note. There is a prophetic gap between verses 5 and 6. After Christ ascended to glory, the Church Age was ushered in and Israel was set aside as a nation. For this reason nothing of Israel's history is depicted here so far as the Church Age is concerned. Verse 6 takes up the picture of Israel again when God begins to deal with His chosen people as a nation. This time is the "70th Week" of Daniel (Dan. 9:24-27), and especially the last half of that week, when Satan turns his hatred and persecution against this people. For this reason we shall reserve verse 6 until the discussion of verses 13-17.

II. THE CONFLICT IN HEAVEN (vv. 7-12)

The story now turns to another phase of the conflict with the dragon, this part in the future. Open war on another one of Israel's fronts is described, as the center of conflict shifts from the earthly scenes to the aerial and stellar regions. Israel's air power is now joined in battle with Satan and his legions during the first half of the tribulation.

1. The conflict in the heavens is described by the word "war" (vv. 7-9). War is a series of engagements lasting over a period of time. It is therefore reasonable to suppose that this extends over the first three and one-half years of the tribulation period. This war is waged between Michael and his angels and Satan and his angels. By comparison with Daniel 12:1 it will be seen that Michael was specially commissioned by God as the guardian of Israel. The occasion for the outbreak of his campaign on the heavenly front is not stated. But by comparing with Daniel 12:2 it can be inferred that the resurrection and rapture of the saints may be the cause. Satan and his angels attempt to prevent the translation of the saints into heaven, and Michael and his angels rush to the rescue (Heb. 1:7, 14; I Thess. 4:16). The war continues for three and one-half years and ends with decisive victory for Michael and his angels (v. 8). Mopping up proceedings follow, and Satan with all his angels is cast out into the earth in the middle of the tribulation period (v. 9).

2. The concern of those in heaven for the inhabitants of the earth is now expressed (vv. 10-12).

(a) A *proclamation* is made by a loud voice in heaven (v. 10). This is an announcement that the first phase of the conflict has been victorious. Satan and his followers have been cast out into the earth, and the kingdom of God is supreme in the three heavens, aerial, stellar, and God's abode. No more can Satan have access to God to accuse the brethren. This announcement is simultaneous with the blowing of the seventh trumpet (11:15), and consists in the taking over of the kingdom of this world by Christ in the heavens. Christ will now initiate a course of events in the earth which will expel the usurpers from the earth during the last three and one-half years of the tribulation.

(b) The *victory* of the saints in the earth will be won at the expense of their lives (vv. 11-12). Satan, now bent on rule or ruin, is incited to great wrath, determined to have his own way at any cost. Heaven recognizes what the power of his fury will mean to the inhabiters of earth. But so great is the power of God among His own, that despite Satan's wrath, the saints overcome him by the blood of the Lamb and the word of their testimony, and so strong and unyielding is their determination that great multitudes pay with their lives.

III. THE CONFLICT IN THE FUTURE (vv. 6, 13-17)

Three great campaigns now take place in the earth, Satan mobilizing all his military might against Israel.

1. The battle of the land (vv. 6, 13-14). When Satan finds himself cast to earth, he turns his venom upon Israel in the land (v. 13). This campaign is launched with the slaughter of the two witnesses in the city of Jerusalem. When Antichrist breaks the covenant with Israel in the middle of the seven-year contract, this signalizes dire peril to the nation. The despicable treatment of the two witnesses and the response of Gentile nations fill all Jews with unspeakable fear. A host of them within the land decide that it is better to flee for their lives than to expose themselves to the hatred of the Beast. So they flee into the wilderness for protection from his wrath. Some people have thought this place is Petra in Edom (v. 6). Sheltered there for three and one-half years Israel experiences protection from the face of the dragon (Matt. 24:15-22; Dan. 11:41). Divine provision is made for her so that in her flight she may elude the hordes of Satan, and so that she may be nourished during those awful days of siege in this mountain fastness (v. 14). The "times," meaning two years, and "time," meaning one year, and "half a time," meaning half a year, add up to three and a half years, the 1,260 days of verse 6 (cf. Exod. 19:4; Dan. 4:16, 23, 25, 32).

2. The battle of the wilderness (vv. 15-16). Not to be deflected from his purpose, Satan, energizing his military genius, the Antichrist, marshals the armies of the world and orders them forth as a flood in pursuit of the fleeing Israelites (cf. Isa. 59:19). For the moment Satan forgets the remnant of Jews who did not flee into the wilderness and are now bottled up in the city of Jerusalem. His entire attention with every bit of military might is focused on the Jews in the wilderness. But despite the overwhelming odds of Antichrist, God comes to the rescue of His own people, and by means of an earthquake swallows up the hordes (v. 16), and leaves Satan and his generalissimo, the Antichrist, in defeat.

3. The battle of the remnant (v. 17). Thwarted again, Satan and his great general, Antichrist, turn back to the land for one last desperate effort to destroy the remnant of Jews in Jerusalem (Zech. 14:1-4). During this final clash the Jews become like David when he fought against Goliath (Zech. 12:8-9). This is the battle of Armageddon, and the victory is won by the glorious appearing of Christ with the armies of heaven (Rev. 19:11-21). The flashing sword of the Spirit from the mouth of Christ is the only weapon necessary for the victory (Dan. 8:25; 11:45).

The defeat of the armies of Antichrist are not described at this point. This is left for later discussion within the Book of Revelation. The proportions of this military organization against the remnant follow in succeeding chapters. The vast preparations of this final move against the Jews is described. The build-up is so huge that it produces the feeling in men of that period and in those who read the story today that no power can possibly stand against it. This makes the final defeat at the hands of the returning Christ the more remarkable.

The Satanic Trinity
in Final Conflict

Revelation 13

THE CHAPTER OUTLINED:

I. The False God, Satan (v. 1)
1. The identification
2. His location
3. The observation

II. The False Christ, Antichrist (vv. 1-10)
1. The person
2. The signs
3. The speech
4. The dominion

III. The False Spirit, the False Prophet (vv. 11-17)
1. The person
2. The signs
3. The power

Chapter 13 of Revelation is another inset which is properly introduced into the story at this point. Its message describes the dimensions of that last great effort of Satan to counterfeit the Holy Trinity and thus deceive the peoples of earth. Nothing in the foregoing millenniums quite approaches in magnitude and method this religious conspiracy. This scheme takes on such grandiose proportions that the major portion of humanity is swept along before it. Since the great tribulation upon Israel has been discussed in chapter 12, it is in order to discuss the methods and the machinations employed by Satan against Israel as a nation and among the Gentiles. In order to give proper perspective to the movement of Satan during the seven years of tribulation, the entire system of evil must be charted from its rise to its final decline.

In its broad lines, the program of Satan for organizing the nations of earth is herein set forth. The satanic trinity counterfeits the divine Trinity and offers to men *the* lie (II Thess. 2:11). At the same time, Satan, through his military genius, Antichrist, organizes the nations for the purpose of controlling the warriors and the wealth of the world. If one has eyes to see, he cannot help but admit there exists already in the twentieth century the groundwork which will shortly blossom forth into the system of Satan. Once the church is caught away from the world to be with Christ, the last hindrance will be removed.

For the sake of convenience in handling the material of this chapter, it will be discussed under three heads: (1) the false God, the great red dragon (v. 1); (2) the false Christ, the first beast, the Antichrist (vv. 1-10); (3) the false spirit, the second beast, the false prophet (v. 11-18).

I. THE FALSE GOD, SATAN (v. 1)

The opening words of the chapter in the King James Version read, "And I stood upon the sand of the sea." The American Standard Version, which is the better rendering, reads, "And he stood upon the sand of the sea." By comparing with verse 17 of the previous chapter it can be seen that the reading of the American Standard Version points to the dragon as the antecedent of the pronoun "he." It is not John who stands upon the sand of the sea, but the dragon. What he sees not only interests him, but also provides for him the opportunity for which he is looking. He is in search of a man who will surrender himself completely to his control.

1. The identification of the dragon has already been made in the previous chapter (12:3, 9; 13:1). He is a dragon, a great fiery monster, brilliant, attractive, formidable (Ezek. 28:12; II Cor. 11:14). He is that old serpent who introduced all the sin, and sorrow, and suffering into this world (Gen. 3:1). He is a devil, a slanderer, and an accuser of the brethren through the centuries (12:10). As Satan, he is the opposer and the adversary of the Lord and His people (Zech. 3:1). By his serpentine methods he has filled the role of deceiver of the nations, being a liar from the beginning and the father of the lie (John 8:44).

2. His location upon the sand of the sea enables him to plan his operations. The sand of the shore doubtless pictures the multiplicity of that which is before him. In referring to the multitudes of people, John says in 20:8, "The number of whom is as the sand of the sea."

3. The observation of this evil genius is a matter of major importance. He sees the sea of the nations in agitation, restless, troubled, in confusion and disorder (Luke 21:25-26; Rev. 17:15). The difficulties and perplexities of the nations attract him, and shortly will provide him with his great opportunity. Being in distress, the nations are in straitened circumstances with ever-narrowing limits of operation. They are suffused with perplexity in that there is a diminishing area of visibility. They experience increasing political and social turbulence as a result of the rising pressures from every direction. This produces an ever-growing physical and emotional disturbance, men's hearts failing them for fear and for looking after those things that are coming upon the earth (Luke 21:25-26). This is Satan's opportunity to put a man in the place of prominence, a man sufficiently great, a superman, in whom the people will place their confidence for peace and security. That man is the beast who rises up out of the sea of the nations.

II. THE FALSE CHRIST, ANTICHRIST (vv. 1-10)

1. The person of the false Christ (vv. 1-2). Let us consider the origination, description, concentration, and organization of this first beast.

(a) His *origination* is out of the sea of the nations, and he is therefore a man. Compare carefully the statement of verse 1 with the statement of verse 18, where it is clearly declared that he is a man. This can only mean that he is some great personality who finally emerges from the milling masses of people. In the desperation and perplexity of the nations this man appears on the horizon as the one who is able to solve the problems of humanity and lead them out of confusion and chaos into order and system and happiness. But while he is a man with great ability, he is one who has some real relationship to the abyss. Twice it is affirmed that he comes out of the abyss (11:7; 17:8). This must mean that he is so much in league with Satan that he is finally indwelt by an evil spirit from the pit and supernaturally energized for his task. His rise is not precipitous. The present tense of the verb "rise" makes clear that it is gradual and progressive. But his revelation to humanity comes with suddenness. The providential movement in the affairs of men brings him with swiftness to the attention of men.

(b) The *description* of this beast is most significant. In *character* he is like a wild beast (cf. 6:8 for meaning of this word). Though he may appear to be the very fullness of perfection as men see him, God knows the nature within, and He identifies him as a wild beast. He possesses a wild, untamed, rebellious nature. In *dimensions* he is both a king and a kingdom. He is expressly called a man (13:18) and is treated as such in other passages (II Thess. 2:3-4; Rev. 19:19-20). He is also described as a king (Rev. 17:10-11; Dan. 8:9, 23). But in addition to these, he is a kingdom. There is no better symbol of a kingdom than the king (Dan. 7:7, 17, 23). The heads of the beast describe the career of empire, the horns refer to the climax of empire in the final confederacy, the crowns denote authority, and the blasphemy marks conspiracy against God (vv. 6; 17:3; II Thess. 2:4).

(c) The *concentration* of all preceding empire in this beast is analyzed by John. The beast was like a leopard, with feet like a bear and a mouth like a lion. By comparison with Daniel 7:3-7 it will be noted that each one of these beasts symbolizes a preceding kingdom: Greece, Medo-Persia, Babylon. This last beast is like all of them put together. Thus this beast sums up in his kingdom all the brilliance of Greece, all the tremendousness of Medo-Persia, and all the autocratic power of Babylon. Such is the revived Roman Empire of the end time.

(d) The *organization* of empire for the beast is unseen and spiritual (v. 2). But though man cannot see it, God can. And so here John is caused to see how Satan has everything arranged for the coming of this mighty man. The dragon gives to this superman his own power, such power as will produce results. The coming of Antichrist is after the working of Satan (II Thess. 2:9). Satan also gives to him his throne or position. A throne is always the symbol of position for the exercise of authority. Satan's throne has been over the nations (Luke 4:5-8). The devil offered this to Christ, but He rejected it. This man will accept the offer. Satan also gives to him authority which is great and will manifest itself in autocratic rule (13:5).

The contrast between Christ and Satan is like the difference between day and night. Christ was meek and humble (Matt. 21:5; Zech. 9:9; Matt. 11:29). But the Antichrist is the personification of arrogance and autocracy (II Thess. 2:4; Dan. 11:36-37). This explains why the eternal Son of God and heir apparent to the throne rejected the offer of Satan. It also explains why the superman of the end time greedily accepts the proffer of Satan.

2. **The signs** of the false Christ (vv. 3-4). You will note here the wounding of the beast, the wondering of the people after him, and the worship of both Satan and the beast.

(a) The *wounding* of one of the heads of this beast is the first matter of importance. The *object* of this wound is the seventh head. The beast, it must be remembered, is a kingdom (Rev. 17:3, 9-10, ASV). This kingdom has seven heads, which are seven mountains, which in turn stand for seven kings. Five of these kings are fallen, one is reigning as John writes, and the seventh king has not yet arrived on the scene. It is this last king and kingdom that is wounded. But the only way the kingdom can be wounded is for its representative or king to be wounded. It is this king that is wounded (13:12), who is a man (13:18). He dies, comes to life again, and thus becomes the eighth king (17:10-11).

The *nature* of his wound is marked by the words "as it were wounded." The American Standard Version reads, "as though it had been smitten" (margin, "slain"). Exactly the same words appear in the original of Revelation 5:6, describing Christ, and are translated "as it had been slain." These words imply the exercise of violence. Without a doubt this is the permitted imitation of the crucifixion of Christ, in order that this man may in every way possible become the great counterfeit of Christ. As Antichrist, he simulates the Christ, stands in the stead of the Christ, and thus stands in opposition to Christ.

The *extent* of his wound has been debated by many. But the translations "to death" (AV) and "unto death" (RV) must mean that he entered into the experience of death. No one doubts that Christ experienced death as a result of His death wound. Why should there be any hesitation here when the same words are used of the wound, and then to this is added the fact that the wound was unto death? This event attracts such worldwide attention that if it is not a wound which produced death, it is so cleverly executed that everyone thinks the Antichrist actually died and rose from the grave. This miracle will produce the exclamation, "Who is like unto the beast? who is able to make war with him?" (Rev. 13:4).

The *cure* of this death-wound is merely stated in this passage, "and his deadly wound was healed" (AV), or, "and his death-stroke was healed" (RV). These words declare that the king of terrors has been conquered.

The slain leader is now raised to life again. The method is not suggested right here. But surely here is the permitted imitation of the resurrection of Christ. This resurrection is not like Christ's, namely, to walk in newness of life and die no more. But neither is it a mere resuscitation. By studying carefully 11:7 and 17:8, 11, it appears that the beast goes into the place of departed spirits at death and then comes up again out of that place. There is no doubt that God permits this in order that men who have rejected the true Christ may believe the lie (II Thess. 2:11).

(b) The *wondering* after the beast and the *worship* of the dragon are the culmination of the ambitions of both Satan and Antichrist (vv. 3-4). For the first time a world that has denied the possibility of physical resurrection in general, and the fact of resurrection in Christ in particular, now awakens to the fact that here is one who has conquered death. In amazement this world shifts its position and believes the lie, the counterfeit, and joins itself to the Antichrist as the invincible warlord. They give the worship to Satan and Antichrist that belong alone to God. "Wondered after the beast" is a phrase that means more than amazement. More specifically these words mean that the multitudes actually follow the Antichrist. They join themselves to him and pledge their allegiance to him.

3. The speech of the false Christ during his reign is now described (vv. 5-6). As to its *nature* two things are asserted of it (v. 5). On the one hand, it is asserted that there was given to him a mouth speaking "great things." This must mean great things from the standpoint of science, philosophy, human wisdom (Dan. 7:8, 20, 25). Here is one to whom the devil has communicated his great wisdom (Ezek. 28:12). If he is indwelt by a demon from the pit, it is altogether possible that some of these great things may come from that source.

On the other hand, he is said to speak "blasphemies." From this man there comes that cold, dispassionate, calm affirmation of untruth about God and the things of God. This will be welcomed by a wicked, Christ-rejecting world. Antichrist will exceed anything by way of blasphemy that has ever been uttered by men (II Thess. 2:10-12).

As to the *period* during which this speech will be uttered, the last three and one-half years of the tribulation will mark its course (v. 5; cf. 11:2-3, 7). And during that period this speech will be directed against the *name of God* and His *people* (v. 6). The truth in the name of God is the deadliest weapon the Antichrist has to face. This truth lingers on in spite of everything he can do to stamp it out. For the first three and one-half years the two witnesses herald this name. The 144,000 preachers in the earth continue to propagate this name, and Antichrist is unable to hinder them. Millions are being saved, even though a great host must pay with their lives for believing the truth.

A great throng of people now in heaven, namely, the church, also become the object of his slander. The truth of the disappearance of this throng from earth by rapture has doubtless swept over the earth, and Antichrist is doing his best to counteract its effect. So now he blasphemes "his tabernacle, even them that dwell in the heaven" (v. 6, ASV; cf. Eph. 2:21-22).

4. The dominion of the false Christ now becomes the matter of discussion (vv. 7-10). The *method* of dominion is by force (v. 7). Armies are mobilized and war is declared against the saints in the earth. This lasts for the remaining period of three and one-half years of tribulation. His dominion is now universal. By this time the other three powers, the northern, eastern, and southern, are subjugated. The northern power has been destroyed by God (Ezek. 38—39). But the eastern and southern have bowed the knee to this king of the west.

The *effect* of this dominion is universal worship (v. 8). By miraculous works and marvelous deeds he attracts the worship of millions (vv. 3-4, 11-15), and by compulsion he gains the worship of many other millions (vv. 16-17).

The *warning* of verses 9 and 10 is in order. A show of force on the part of the saints will be to no avail. It were better to trust the Lord and endure hardship, knowing that the reign of this tyrant will soon come to an end. A show of force may only make retaliation in force more severe.

III. THE FALSE SPIRIT, THE FALSE PROPHET (vv. 11-17)

1. The person described here as the second beast has a relationship to the first beast that simulates the relation of the Holy Spirit to Christ (vv. 11-12). He *originates* "out of the earth." Some think "earth" refers to a more settled condition of things (religious) than the term "sea" (13:1). On the other hand, this term may be taken literally and mean out of the abyss. Hence this may be an evil spirit taking up its residence in a man.

This person is *described* as a wild beast, as in the previous case. The two horns like a lamb suggest religious power. But he speaks like a dragon. Since this does not have to do with appearance, it must refer to his message. With all the religious subtlety of the serpent through the centuries, this beast propagates a message of religious delusion (II Cor. 11:13-15; 4:4).

His *organization* is definitely related to and derived from both the dragon and the first beast (v. 12). His authority comes from the first beast and is therefore just like it. His position is under, or before, the first beast. This beast is the counselor and prime minister for Antichrist. His purpose is to turn all devotion and worship toward Antichrist. And he has force at his command to compel devotion to the first beast.

2. **The signs** displayed by this beast are religious in character (vv. 13-15). The religious character of these signs can be noted by comparison with other passages (vv. 13, 15). There is first the sign of fire from heaven (v. 13; Mal. 3:2; 4:1). There is also the sign of life (v. 15; John 7:28; 6:40). The word "life" in the original Greek is the word for spirit. This probably means that the false prophet causes an evil spirit to inhabit the image and speak out through the image. By means of these lying wonders he is able to deceive men. The result of this religious revival instigated and directed by the false prophet is a return to idolatrous worship. The worship of one who is nothing more than man is a return to pure paganism.

It should be understood, however, that miracles alone are not sufficient to turn people in the direction of paganism. There must be a conditioning philosophy that has prepared the way. And this will be the case in relation to the Antichrist. There will be on the one hand the negative aspect of turning away from faith in a supernatural and transcendent God (II Thess. 2:3), and there will be on the other hand the positive aspect of creating a pantheizing mythology (II Tim. 4:3-4). These miracles will merely serve as the immediate occasion and confirmation of the philosophy.

3. **The power** of the second beast to compel obedience to his commands is tremendous (vv. 16-17). With the wealth of the world concentrated in his hands he is able to perform feats that would otherwise be impossible.

(a) *Public identification and regimentation* is the chief design of the mark men are compelled to wear (v. 16). This is undoubtedly another counterfeiting of the things of God. Since God sealed a group of people to indicate ownership and allegiance (7:1-8), so now Antichrist also determines to bring every last being out into the open so rebellion can be detected and stamped out. No exceptions are made to this marking. All classes of society are included. The most conspicuous parts of the body are used for the mark, either the forehead or the right hand.

(b) *Self-preservation and operation* is the force that compels men to submit to this marking (v. 17). Having a commercial monopoly on the wealth of the world, the false prophet is able to compel all men to bow the knee to his demands. If they want to live, they must receive the mark, and bear the name or the number of the first beast. Extreme need drives men into the camp of the Antichrist. Only those who love not their lives unto death, and that because they have the mark of Christ upon them in salvation, will resist this tyranny of the end time. A system of rationing, the most absolute in the history of mankind, will be inaugurated. Nineteenth and twentieth century civilization brought with it the conscription of armies and the mobilization of all the resources of nations in order to wage modern warfare. Rationing of supplies was one of the features. Governmental control of industry and commerce was another. And ration stamps was another. Antichrist will need to organize and implement on an even larger scale and in a more restrictive sense. The mark of the beast will be his method of implementation.

Conclusion (v. 18). Wisdom is in these words. No one who has gone before has been the Antichrist. Saints of the end time either just before or just after the coming of Christ may need this word of encouragement. But 666 is the number of a man. Let no one be deceived.

9

The Zion Vision, the Harvest, and the Seven Vials

Revelation 14, 15, 16

THE CHAPTER OUTLINED:

I. The Zion Vision and the Harvest (Chap. 14)
  1. The firstfruits
  2. The further fruits
  3. The final issues

II. The Seven Angels and the Bowls of Wrath (Chaps. 15-16)
  1. The portrayal of judgment
  2. The preparation for judgment
  3. The pouring out of judgment
  4. The purpose of the judgment
  5. The perfecting of judgment

After the blowing of the seventh trumpet in the midst of the tribulation week (11:15), a series of insets were introduced into the text to enlarge upon some of the features that would otherwise remain obscure. Chapter 12 recorded the horrible, age-long persecution of Israel by Satan, the dragon. The final organization of the satanic trinity against God and the saints was set forth in chapter 13. The dreadful gloom that descends upon the scene leaves John and the reader in despair. In order to let some rays of light through into the midst of this appalling darkness, another inset is introduced into the story consisting of a series of prophetic visions and announcements (chap. 14). At this point we return to the regular chronological unfolding of the book when the seven vials of God's wrath begin and run their course (chaps. 15–16).

The information of chapter 14, like that of other insets, is introduced at the proper point in the story, with its time sequence running both backward and forward. The time element of chapter 14 is exactly like that of chapters 7 and 13. It takes the reader back to the beginning of the tribulation week and runs forward to the end of the week. In this chapter the reader is made to realize that despite the fact that Satan is launching his most powerful attack upon God and His people, God is also organized and is working at the same time to offset the workings of the satanic trinity.

In chapter 14 it will be noted that there comes first a vision of the firstfruits to God and the Lamb (vv. 1-5). This is followed by a vision of the further fruits to God and the Lamb (vv. 6-13). The chapter concludes with the final issues in the defeat of the wicked (vv. 14-20).

I. THE ZION VISION AND THE HARVEST (chap. 14)

1. The firstfruits to the Lamb (vv. 1-5). The scene is located on Mount Zion (v. 1), then comes the song from heaven (vv. 2-3), and finally one notes the service of the redeemed (vv. 4-5).

(a) The *scene* on Mount Zion (v. 1). The mountain is the well-known one to Jews, the city of Jerusalem in the earth, and not the heavenly Jerusalem (Heb. 12:22; cf. Zech. 14:1 and following). There is no reason to suppose that this scene should be located anywhere else. The Lamb is standing on this mount, which is a prophetic forecast of the coming of Christ in glory as recorded in chapter 19 of this book and referred to elsewhere in the Bible (Zech. 14:1 and following; Matt. 25:31 and following). With Christ on the mount is a company of saints numbering 144,000, with the name of the heavenly Father written on their foreheads. This is the same company who was saved and sealed, according to Revelation 7:1-8. The seal is here spoken of as the Father's name. This may be the outward manifestation of the Holy Spirit (Eph. 1:13; 4:30), for it is altogether possible that there is something visible to the eye.

(b) The *song* from heaven (vv. 2-3). Out of heaven comes a voice with tremendous range, like that of many waters. It rolls and peals and echoes like thunder, and gathering volume it finally individualizes into the voice of many harpers playing on their harps. This is the song over the redeemed of earth, a gospel song of emotional rejoicing and gratitude. This is a song with freshness in it. It is new and strong and vivacious. The message is old, but the impulse is new for the 144,000 redeemed souls have provided the occasion for the melody before the heavenly audience of living creatures, the twenty-four elders, and the Holy Trinity. Though the 144,000 do not sing the song, they are the only ones who can learn it, because none but the redeemed can understand the joy that salvation brings.

(c) The *service* of the redeemed (vv. 4-5). Certain things qualify this group for service. *Spiritual* qualities are present. On the negative side they are separated from evil, since it says they have not been defiled with women. While this probably has first reference to spiritual chastity, yet it may and probably does refer in a more literal sense to separation from sexual immorality, for idolatry has always been associated with such. The apostasy of the end time and the subtle pantheizing philosophy conditioning the thinking of mankind prepare the way for the descent into idolatry and the consequent immorality such as existed in the days of Noah and Lot. Therefore it is very much in order to make reference to the fact that these have not defiled themselves with women. It will be a marvel of God's grace that in the midst of the miasma of corruption there will be a company of saints. Being called virgins doubtless relates this group to those of Matthew 25:1-13 who will be ready to accompany Christ into His kingdom. On the positive side, it is asserted that this redeemed company follows Christ whithersoever He goes. This is further evidence that the grace of God is sufficiently powerful to enable saved people to live lives of holiness in the midst of the most intensely sinful surroundings.

This group also possesses certain *judicial* qualities that enable them for service. By redemption they have been brought into this new relationship with Christ. The very price of Christ's blood has protected them from the wrath being poured out upon the earth (7:1-8). To make this effective they have been marked with a seal. But besides this, they constitute a firstfruits to God and the Lamb for the coming kingdom. Firstfruits always imply that there will be further fruits. This means that many more Jews and Gentiles will yet be saved during the tribulation period and prepared to enter the millennial kingdom. It is interesting to note that the unnumbered multitude follow in Revelation 7:9-17, the sheep follow the story of the virgins in Matthew 25:31-46, and a similar situation prevails in this chapter (vv. 6-13). As the sad decline in the salvation of men is viewed today, and it would almost appear that the purpose of God is being thwarted, believers need to get a glimpse of the future through the light of prophecy. They will then learn that the church is just one company of the saved, and other companies will yet be saved (Acts 15:14-17), among which are Jews and Gentiles during the tribulation period.

Special characteristics, *doctrinal* in meaning, qualify these redeemed people for service. The American Standard Version reads, "And in their mouth was found no lie: they are without blemish" (v. 5). This must mean that there was no false confession in their mouths. In that day when many are believing "the lie" and giving assent by open allegiance to Antichrist, these people do not fall into this error. In this respect they are without blemish, and are qualified to go forth during the last half of the tribulation period as preachers of the everlasting Gospel.

In a day when philosophical and doctrinal confusion will be rampant it will be of special importance that the testimony of some be clear and uncorrupted, so that their ministry may be effective to the millions of men all across the world. It is during this period that the Gospel will be preached to the ends of the earth (Matt. 24:14; Mark 13:10). It is this preaching of the Gospel that will bring the harvest of souls for the populating of the kingdom during the Millennium.

2. The further fruits to the Lamb (vv. 6-13). Proclamations of the everlasting Gospel, of the fall of Babylon, of the doom of beast worshipers, and of salvation for the saints now follow.

(a) The proclamation of the *everlasting Gospel* (vv. 6-7). An angel is seen carrying this message. But this probably only suggests haste. The angel doubtless delivers the message to the 144,000 who will do the actual preaching. By comparison with Revelation 1:1 this is a legitimate conclusion. Such was true in the case of the Law (Gal. 3:19; Heb. 2:2). The message is proclaimed everywhere, which sounds very much like the account in Revelation 7:9-17. This message is good news with emphasis on Christ's coming in glory. It heralds the coming kingdom, which is announced by the seventh trumpet (11:15). It is now time to fear God, for He alone deserves worship, and when men fail to give Him what is due, judgment will fall upon them.

(b) The proclamation of the *fall of Babylon* (v. 8). Another angel now announces the fall of Babylon. This is a prophetic glimpse of what is to follow. Twice the word "fallen" appears. It refers to chapters 17 and 18 of this book. The religious system of chapter 17 falls in the midst of the tribulation week with the blowing of the seventh trumpet. This judgment is providential, because it is wrought by Antichrist and his confederates upon the great false religious system, the harlot church of the end time. From then on Antichrist himself becomes the religious system; he and his city meet their doom, according to chapter 18, near the end of the tribulation week. But this judgment upon the city comes directly from God just prior to the coming of Christ in Glory.

(c) The proclamation of *doom to beast worshipers* (vv. 9-11). Still another angel makes this solemn announcement. Beast worshipers shall drink of the wrath of God (Rev. 19:15). They shall go immediately into Hades, where they will be confined for one thousand years until the Great White Throne judgment (Rev. 20:11-15). Their torment there will be exactly like that in the lake of fire except that it will be temporary. But after their resurrection for judgment at the Great White Throne, they shall be cast into the lake of fire and their confinement there will be for all eternity.

If it is remembered at which point this proclamation is made, it will become clear why this word of explanation is needed. At the moment Antichrist comes to the apex of his career and is crowned the head over all nations of the world, his worshipers will be enjoying their greatest prosperity and prominence. It will seem that their well-being and affluence are the clear demonstration that they made the right decision and are following the path of true wisdom. But it only seems that way at the middle of the tribulation week. Since God alone knows the future, this prophetic proclamation is an encouragement to the saints who must face the rigors of persecution that lie immediately ahead.

(d) The proclamation of *salvation to the saints* (vv. 12-13). A voice from heaven now speaks (v. 13). The message is reassuring. Millions join Antichrist during this terrible period of tribulation. But the true saints persist in faith through all of it. They keep the commandments of God, and they hold to their faith in Christ, sure evidence that faith is as powerful as ever. And if they die, and many will, they die in the Lord, demonstrating that they possess a blessed nature. Their recompense begins immediately, for they rest from the pains of persecution, and reward for their works greets them.

3. The final issues in the defeat of Satan (vv. 14-20). As John looks he sees a vision of the harvest coming at the close of the tribulation perod. While there appear to be two reapings, there is in reality only one (cf. Matt. 13:36-43). Christ is the Lord of the harvest, and the angels are the reapers.

(a) The *Son of Man* and the reaping (vv. 14-16). The appearance of the Son of Man is clearly one symbolizing judgment. The white cloud is the cloud of glory which constitutes the proper environment of deity. The golden crown marks His sovereignty and promise of power. And the sickle is the symbol of harvest and approaching judgment. All judgment has been committed unto the Son (John 5:22). Out of the temple, the proper source and surety of judgment, the angel comes and commands Christ to thrust in the sickle. The cup of iniquity is full, the harvest is ripe, and the hour of judgment has come. Christ thrusts in the sickle and the earth is reaped.

(b) The *other angel* and the reaping (vv. 17-20). The angelic reaper from the temple now acts as the agent of Christ (cf. Matt. 13:39-43). From the altar, the place of judgment, an announcing angel which has power over fire orders the reaping angel to thrust in the sickel. The clusters of the vine of the earth, all those who are joined to Satan and Antichrist, are now gathered to Jerusalem in the valley just outside the city. This becomes the winepress where the wrath of God is poured out without mixture. This is the valley of Jehoshaphat, the vale of Esdraelon, one hundred sixty miles in length. Armies of the nations gather here at the command of Antichrist (Zech. 14:1-4; Joel 3:10-14). And Christ at His coming in glory treads the winepress (Isa. 63:1-6; Rev. 19:11-21).

There are several very significant things appearing in this passage. First, there is a *time* for harvest. The word used in this passage is "hour" in the original Greek (v. 15). This draws the matter of harvest to a focal point. In the parable of the wheat and tares this is called the end of the age (Matt. 13:39). Second, there is the crop to be harvested. In this passage it is designated as "the harvest of the earth" (v. 15), and "the vine of the earth" (v. 18). In the parable of the wheat and tares this crop is named "tares . . . the children of the wicked one" (Matt. 13:38). Third, the reason for harvest lies in the fact that the inherent nature of the crop has not passed through the process of development to full ripeness (vv. 15, 18). Fourth, the method of harvesting is by means of judgment and removal from the present scenes (vv. 18-19; Matt. 13:40-42). The righteous are left to shine forth in the kingdom of their Father (Matt. 13:43). This event differs from the rapture of the church, which occurs seven years earlier when Christ comes and catches away the righteous from the earth.

II. THE SEVEN ANGELS AND THE BOWLS OF WRATH (chaps. 15—16)

By examining each set of seven, the seals, trumpets, and vials, it will be discovered that each is preceded by an introductory vision. Chapters 4 and 5 are introductory to the seals, chapter 8:1-6 to the trumpets, and chapter 15 to the vials. The vision in every case is in heaven. For convenience chapters 15 and 16 will be divided into five portions for study.

1. The portrayal of judgment upon the world (15:1-4). A sign in heaven, a sea of glass, and the song of Moses are described. The sign consists of seven angels having the seven last plagues in which God's wrath is finished. Wrath approached in 6:17, and it is now finished (15:1). The sea of glass in the heavenly temple was the pattern for the molten sea in the earthly temple (I Kings 7:23). This sea is closely akin to the Red Sea in the experiences of Israel. Being mingled with fire, it symbolizes judgment. The sea is covered with a victorious company who have prevailed over the beast, his image, mark, number and name. Like the Israelites of old at the Red Sea, they sing the song of Moses and the Lamb, a song of victory, ascribing greatness, justice, truth, and holiness to God because His judgments are now manifest.

2. The preparation for judgment on the world (15:5-8). The most holy place in the temple is opened. There is the ark of the testimony. The ark signifies that God is faithful in keeping covenant and promise. Since the temple is God's dwelling place, out of the temple come the seven last plagues. The angels are the agents to execute this wrath. The number seven is the number of completeness. Their white clothing speaks of judgment without mercy, and their golden girdles announce the righteousness of their task. The seven bowls of wrath committed into the hands of the angels are full to overflowing. Judgment comes from the presence of God just as does salvation, and is the reverse side of salvation. Since men are hardened in sin, and like Pharaoh have challenged God, God does not permit anyone to enter the temple until the period of wrath has run its course. During this period there will be no salvation (16:9, 11, 21).

3. The pouring out of judgment on the earth (16:1-7). After the announcement and command for the angels to pour out the bowls of wrath upon the earth, the first three bowls are emptied in quick succession (v. 1).

(a) The *first vial* of wrath is poured out upon the earth (v. 2). It takes the form of a grievous sore, rotten and incurable, and affects all those who worship the beast, wear his mark, or bow down to his image.

(b) The *second vial* of wrath falls upon the sea and affects the waters universally (v. 3). In appearance the sea becomes like blood, and it actually congeals like blood. The result is that all life in the sea dies. Since the world of that coming day has turned to violence and the shedding of blood, God gives them their fill. This indicates that the farther men drift from God, the less concern they have for life as well as for truth. In this environment of violence, life will be most precarious.

(c) The *third vial* is poured out upon the fountains of waters (vv. 4-7). They too become like blood. There is no reason why we should not accept this statement as literal truth. The justice of this judgment is declared by two angels (vv. 5, 7). It lies in the fact that the wicked are having measured to them exactly what they have meted out. They have shed innocent blood. Now God gives them blood to drink (v. 6).

4. The purpose of the judgment on the world (16:8-16). The fourth, fifth, and sixth vials are now poured out. It is evident by the response which comes from men that they have become confirmed in sin, and this is the reason or purpose for judgment.

(a) The *fourth vial* is poured out upon the sun (vv. 8-9). The heat of the sun is increased until it scorches men. But the response of men shows how hardened they are in sin. Though they suffer excruciating pain, and know the course of it, they blaspheme God and refuse to repent and give God the glory.

(b) The *fifth vial* is poured out upon the seat of the beast (vv. 10-11). The concentration of wrath is now upon the very throne of the beast, the one whom the peoples of earth are worshiping. His kingdom is filled with darkness so great that it produces terrible sores and horrible pain. Though the pain is almost unendurable, and men gnaw their tongues, they blaspheme God and refuse to repent of their deeds.

(c) The *sixth vial* is poured out upon the river Euphrates (vv. 12-16). As a result it is dried up and opens the way for the kings of the east to move westward. The satanic trinity now begins to organize for the final battle. Demons, evil spirits, go forth from the mouth of each of the three leaders to gather the nations in to Palestine for the great day of God almighty. This will be the battle of Armageddon. It is described in 14:17-20 and also in 19:11-21. God permits these plans of Antichrist to go unhindered, for by means of this gathering of armies the stage is being set for the final outpouring of His wrath. Little does Satan realize here that his own wisdom is corrupted, and God is actually using this evil scheme to prepare the way for the day when he will deliver the final death blow to the satanic kingdom. All who dwell in the earth are warned of this coming day of wrath and urged to be ready by keeping their garments and avoiding nakedness.

5. **The perfecting of judgment** upon the earth (16:17-21). The seventh vial brings to a grand climax the wrath of God upon a sinful world.

This vial is poured out upon the air (v. 17). This is due perhaps to the fact that the air is filled with hosts of wicked spirits. The announcement is then made that judgment is done, finished, brought to an end. The judgment is universal in effect. The greatest earthquake ever felt in the earth takes place. The great city Babylon is divided into three parts. All the other cities of the world fall. The islands of the sea and the mountains of earth are affected. This probably brings about a readjustment of the earth's surface. From the air a great hail falls upon wicked men, and none remain. The size of the hail is about one hundred pounds for each stone. This judgment comes near the end. But the result of the sixth vial runs to the absolute end of the tribulation.

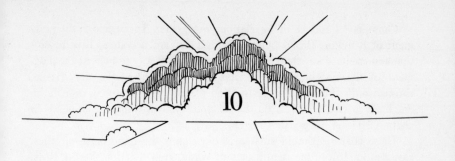

10

The Doom
of the Scarlet Woman
and the City of Babylon

Revelation 17 and 18

THE CHAPTER OUTLINED:

    I. The Judgment of the Great Whore (Chap. 17)
       1. The victim of judgment
       2. The visitor of judgment
       3. The visitation of judgment

   II. The Judgment of Babylon the Great (Chap. 18)
       1. The proclamation of judgment
       2. The lamentation of judgment
       3. The visitation of judgment

Chapters 17 and 18 of Revelation go together. The theme is the judgment of Babylon. This Babylon is both a city and a system. It is the city that represents the system. Therefore, the easiest way to present the judgment of the system is by describing the judgment of the city. Hence, through both chapters, the destruction of the city is featured, though the emphasis in chapter 17 is on the religious system, while the emphasis in chapter 18 is on the political system.

These chapters should enlarge in our minds the importance of cities. One cannot ignore the significance of Washington, London, Berlin, Paris, Moscow, Tokyo, Jerusalem. In the end time Babylon will be the city toward which all the nations of earth will be looking. Out of that city will go forth the decrees that control the nations in their religious observances (17:2, 5, 18). And no less prominent will be this city in its political and commercial overlordship of the nations (18:2-3).

Cities originated with Cain, the evil son of Adam and Eve (Gen. 4:17). He called the first city after his son Enoch. Amazing but true, evil men have been attracted to cities throughout the course of the world's history. It must be that sin thrives best in society and misery loves company. Holiness can flourish in blessed concourse with God alone. But sin is denial of God and rebellion against Him. It leaves man in absolute loneliness apart from the company of other men.

Babylon was originally built by Nimrod for the purpose of defying God (Gen. 10:8-10; 11:1-9). Ancient lore says that Semiramis was the wife of Nimrod. She was the foundress of the Babylonian mysteries and the first high priestess of idolatry. The false religion became the fountainhead of idolatry and the mother of all the pagan systems of the world. Its fullest development will come in the Babylon of the end time.

Semiramis bore a son whom she declared was miraculously conceived. When presented to the people, he was hailed as the promised deliverer. He was named Tammuz (Ezek. 8:14). The rites of his worship were secret. Only the initiated were permitted to know its mysteries. It was Satan's effort to delude mankind with an imitation of the truth. Within a thousand years this spread throughout the world. The symbols were all the same, although under different names, such as Isis and Horus, Aphrodite and Eros, Venus and Cupid.

The identity of this Babylon of the end time is difficult to point out. Many Bible scholars insist that old Babylon will be rebuilt. Others are just as strong in their insistence that Rome is the Babylon of the end time. It seems quite clear that the fourth world empire of Daniel 2, the Roman

Empire, will be revived in the last days. Most certainly the political greatness of Babylon was transferred to this fourth kingdom. But this does not mean that Rome, the capital city of that day, may not be relocated in these closing days. In fact, there is good reason to believe that Babylon, which was once the fountainhead of empire and false religion, will in the end time flourish again in even a greater way, and there judgment will come upon the system in the very place it originated.

There are a number of reasons why it is perfectly sound to conclude that there will be a city in the end time located near the site of the old city of Babylon, and that this city will be named Babylon. In the first place, the Scriptures use the name Babylon. For those who take the Scripture literally, it is difficult to escape this conclusion. In the second place, even though Old Testament prophecy declares that the old city of Babylon will not be rebuilt, this could still be true, and the end time city could be built near by. Such a prophecy was uttered concerning Jericho, yet there was a New Testament Jericho built not far away, and there is a modern Jericho in still a different location, though not far from the ancient site. In the third place, it was the habit of great monarchs to want cities of their own building for their capitals. The pride and arrogance of Antichrist will exceed that of any monarch ever to precede him. It is therefore possible he will want his own city. In the fourth place, with modern machinery to speed the task, there is no physical reason why a world capital could not be built somewhere on the plains of Shinar in the Middle East.

I. THE JUDGMENT OF THE GREAT WHORE (chap. 17)

The key verse of chapter 17 is verse 1. It centers attention on the religious system of Babylon. In words that are so clear that one cannot misunderstand, the angel shows John "the judgment of the great whore."

As has already been pointed out in the Book of Revelation, the figure of a woman is used to symbolize religion. Jezebel represents the pagan idolatry of the past (2:20), the sun-clothed woman represents Israel (12:1), the bride of Christ represents the church (21:9; 19:7-8), and the great whore represents the false church, all apostate religion after the true church has been translated (19:2).

The judgment of the great whore is a providential judgment of God brought upon apostate religion. God does not execute this judgment directly, but rather uses the Antichrist and the ten kings to perform it. This takes place when the Antichrist comes to the zenith of his power in the midst of the week (Rev. 17:12, 16-17). Having gained his objective by using false religion, he is then done with it, and he exalts himself to the place of deity and worship for the last three and one-half years of the tribulation period.

By comparison, it will be seen that chapters 17 and 19 are an expansion of the seventh vial (16:17-21), while chapter 19 is an expansion of the sixth vial (16:12-16).

1. The victim of judgment, the great whore (17:1-6). The judgment of the great whore is the destruction of a religious system (vv. 1-2). Moreover, this religious system is localized and centered in a city (vv. 5, 18). This means that this great religious system has moved the office of its government to the capital city of the world empire. Since the Bible speaks of seven mountains on which the woman sits, it is easy to identify this harlot with the Roman Catholic Church. But the fact is these mountains have to do with empire, and this religious system is far greater than the Roman Catholic system. This great ecclesiastical organization of the end time is universal in scope and includes all segments of Catholicism: Roman, Russian, and Greek; it includes all segments of liberal and apostate Protestantism together with the vast array of cults; it includes apostate Judaism and the great pagan religions of the world. It will probably be true that Roman Catholicism will provide the outward superstructure and organization for this great composite of false religion, for it is the most highly developed system in the world. The trend now in evidence within all segments of organized religion causes one to look more sharply at the meaning of this chapter.

(a) The *scope* of influence covered by the great whore is worldwide, for it is written that she "sitteth upon many waters" (vv. 1, 15). The description of verse 15 is a way of indicating universality, and religion is universal.

(b) The *nature* of her influence is suggested by the words, "the wine of her fornication" (v. 2). Political powers have joined with her in unholy relation for the sake of existence, and peoples have drunk so deeply of this wine that they are drunken. In their drunken stupor they lose all sense of balance, perspective, and reality.

(c) The *power* of her influence is suggested by the fact that she sits "upon a scarlet coloured beast" (v. 3). Having turned aside from the green pastures provided by the Lord, she is now in the wilderness or desert. But so great is her power that Antichrist permits this harlot to ride him for the sake of the advantage he will gain in his bid for power during the first three and one-half years of the tribulation. Nevertheless, the power of false religion over the state is supreme. And from the state, religion receives financial, political and military protection.

(d) The *wealth* of her influence is marked by the fact that she is "decked with gold and precious stones" (v. 4). She is arrayed in purpose, suggesting royalty; clothed in scarlet, marking the attractiveness of the system; decked with jewels, indicating the wealth she has gained in religious traffic; and holding a cup full of abominations and filthiness, all that she has to offer to the millions of her devotees.

(e) The *mystery* of her influence is clearly stated: "Mystery, Babylon the Great" (v. 5). Secrecy has always been associated with false religion and remains to the end the one lure which people have not been able to escape. This harlot has mothered the whole brood of abominations that have swarmed through the earth.

(f) The *results* of her influence are appalling. She is "drunken with the blood of the saints" (v. 6). She made the Old Testament saints pay with their lives. The New Testament witnesses for Christ also fell under her violence. But the colossal proportions of her persecution during the first half of the tribulation will exceed anything known to man. This is what amazes the Apostle John.

2. The visitor of judgment, the Antichrist (vv. 7-15). The angel acting as John's guide enquires the reason for his amazement, and assures him that he will explain the mystery of the woman and the beast that carries her (v. 7).

(a) The *identity* of the beast is the first matter of explanation (v. 8). He is the first beast of chapter 13. As in the former chapter, he has seven heads and ten horns (v. 7). He makes war with the saints (11:7; 13:7). He is wondered at by those whose names are not in the book of life (13:3-4; 17:8). He is the beast that was, and is not, and yet is (13:3; 11:7; 17:8). And he is both a kingdom and a person (17:9-11).

(b) The *career* of the beast is marked by the course of empire (v. 11). The seven heads are seven mountains, and mountains refer to governments or kingdoms. In many passages of the Old Testament the figure of a mountain is used to symbolize a government. Some passages denote the government of God (Isa. 2:2; 11:9; 30:29; Dan. 2:35), while others refer to the governments of men (Amos 4:1; 6:1). In this passage of Revelation the mountains cannot refer to heaps of material stuff. Two things forbid such interpretation. First, the better translation of the American Standard Version declares of the mountains: "And they are seven kings" (v. 10). Second, their existence has to do with time and not space. "Five are fallen, and one is, and the other is not yet come" (v. 10). In addition to these two things, the seventh mountain is personalized and referred to by the pronoun "he" (v. 10). Perhaps the seven great kingdoms of history are in mind here: Egypt, Assyria, Babylon, Medo-Persia, Greece, Rome, and revived Rome. Besides being kingdoms, these are represented by seven kings (v. 10, ASV). The beast, Antichrist, is the seventh. He dies and comes to life again and thus becomes the eighth.

(c) The *climax* of the beast is marked by alliance with ten kings, who in that revived Roman Empire join together with Antichrist (vv. 12-13). This is the meaning of the ten horns.

(d) The *culmination* of this alliance with the ten kings is war (v. 14). But this war is ultimately against the Lamb, and the Lamb overcomes this confederacy of the end time. The final battle of this conflict is recorded in Revelation 19. Not only is it declared that the beast and the ten kings make war with the Lamb (17:14), but also all the other kings of the earth under the leadership of the beast (19:19). There are two ways of explaining this. The easiest is to conclude that making war with Israel is making war against the Lamb. The other is to take the text literally. In this case it could mean that the pride and self-sufficiency of Antichrist has reached such heights that he imagines he can actually ascend the heavens and fight against the Son of God. In the light of present scientific invention and human ambition, this might not be far from the meaning of the text.

(e) The *sway* of the beast and the woman is worldwide (v. 15). All peoples and tongues and tribes and nations are included.

3. The visitation of judgment, the whore destroyed (vv. 16-18). In these verses it is demonstrated how God permits one evil power to destroy another and thus perform His will.

(a) The *ultimate source* of this destruction of the whore is the fact that God has put it into the hearts of the ten kings to destroy her (v. 17). This is not an immediate, but a providential, judgment of God. Once God's will has been carried out, later He will destroy the ten kings along with Antichrist.

(b) The *immediate source* of judgment is the hatred of the ten kings (v. 16). This means that the beast and his vassal kings only submit to the domination of false religion that they might gain their own ends. There is no love between them. Each is using the other as a tool. When opportunity arrives, the ten kings destroy the woman.

(c) The *essential nature* of the judgment is significant (v. 16). The woman is made "desolate," meaning that all political and commercial support is withdrawn, and she stands absolutely alone. Shorn of her support, she is "naked." All the outward display that made her so attractive is taken away, and she has nothing to hide her from the gazing multitude, nothing to obscure the vision, nothing to distort the absolute truth. The kings "eat her flesh" in the sense of confiscating the vast stores of wealth she has accumulated through the years. And they "burn her with fire," thus bringing complete destruction and abolition of religion, which is the proper end for a harlot (Lev. 21:9). Worship is turned to Satan and his false Christ, which has been his supreme ambition through the millenniums (Rev. 13:4; II Thess. 2:3-4).

As a final reminder, the reader is informed that the woman is that great city which reigns over the kings of the earth (v. 18). While this is a religious system, it is also a city that represents the whole system.

II. THE JUDGMENT OF BABYLON THE GREAT (chap. 18)

The reader needs to be reminded that the key to this chapter is in verse 2. It states that "Babylon the great is fallen." In verse 10, 16, 18-19, and 21 it is the judgment upon the city that is emphasized. The judgment upon the city takes place "after these things" (v. 1), that is, after the destruction of the great whore. Whereas the destruction of the whore was wrought by the Antichrist and the ten kings (17:16-17), and in this sense was judgment through secondary causes, the judgment of the city of Babylon is executed by God himself (v. 8) and is not a providential judgment as in the previous case, but is one direct "from heaven" (v. 1).

The intimations of the judgment upon the city have already been given. An angelic proclamation recorded in 14:8 and the pouring out of the seventh vial (16:19) both pointed to this event. The first (14:8) emphasized the double aspect of judgment both as a religious system and a political power. The second (16:19) stressed the utter destruction of the city The double aspect is also mentioned again in this chapter (18:6), the first of which has already taken place, while the second is about to be experienced.

It must be repeated that the identity of this city is difficult. As far as present day history is concerned, it looks as though Rome is the place. But we must not overlook the fact that in this day of industrialization it would not be difficult to rebuild the city of Babylon and shift the scenes to some site near Babylon on the Euphrates. The prophecy of Zechariah suggests that evil will be removed to that location and will be judged in the place of its origin (Zech. 5:5-11). One dare not overlook the fact that even today the eyes of the nations are turning again to the Middle East. The gigantic stores of oil in that region, to say nothing of the vast stores of wealth in other respects, may be a deciding factor in the end time. There is a sense in which that is a strategic geographical location in relation to the entire world. One thing is certain: Jerusalem, located in the Middle East, is going to be the center of divine government throughout the Millennium.

1. The proclamation of judgment (vv. 1-8). Another great angel comes down from heaven with great power (v. 1). His glory is so brilliant that the entire earth is lighted by it. This is the angel that makes the proclamation of judgment.

(a) The *desolation* of Babylon is pictured as utter destruction (v. 2). The city is fallen and has become the habitation of demons and the cage for unclean and hateful birds.

(b) The *fornication* of the city with the inhabitants of earth is the reason for judgment (v. 3). The commercial wealth of the city has drawn merchants from near and far. Her political power has attracted kings. Such intimate relations with the city caused the peoples of earth to share in her sins, and they must now also share in her judgment.

(c) *Separation* from the city is the only means of escaping its judgment (v. 4). "Come out of her, my people," is the cry of the Lord to the Jews and thousands more who have been lured into this city.

(d) *Retribution* upon Babylon is twofold (vv. 5-6). The highest form of satanic defiance is indicated by the statement that her sins have reached to heaven. Though God did not seem to exist when Babylon was ascending the ladder of fame, He did not forget; and when the hour strikes, He rewards her double. The religious system is already destroyed (chap. 17), and the political power is about to suffer a like fate (chap. 18).

(e) *Exaltation,* when it comes from self, is short-lived (v. 7). This city glorified herself, lived deliciously, meted out sorrow and torment to others, and dared to boast that she was a queen and no widow and would never see sorrow. This self-sufficiency and independence are double reasons why she should be destroyed.

(f) *Termination* of her power comes in a day (v. 8). The suddenness of it; the intensity of the plagues, death, and mourning; the extremity of it, utterly burned with fire; the sovereignty of it; God being the one who judged her: all produce consternation in those who view the result.

2. The lamentation over judgment (vv. 9-19). It is almost unbelievable the effect this has upon the populace of earth.

(a) The *governmental* authorities lament her fate (vv. 9-10). The fornication and luxury afforded by this city are cut off forever.

(b) *Commercial* officials bemoan her destruction (vv. 11-16). Their source of gain, which included everything from gold to the souls of men, is gone.

(c) *Transportational* personnel lament her fall (vv. 17-19). Their hope of gain is also gone. They grew rich just transporting goods to and from the city.

3. The visitation of judgment (vv. 20-24).

(a) The *vengeance* of divine judgment is done; therefore, heaven and its inhabitants can now rejoice (v. 20).

(b) The *violence* of this judgment brings complete destruction (vv. 21-23). A stone falls upon the city. This stone is the Lord Jesus himself (Dan. 2:34-35, 44-45). When it falls upon the city it produces catastrophic results. So complete is the destruction that the refrain "no more at all" is spoken of everything about the city.

(c) This judgment is the *vindication* of God and all those who had to suffer at the hands of this power (v. 24). The blood of the prophets found within the city showed that this city had rejected God and His message and had hated good men.

The Marriage in Heaven and the Supper on Earth

Revelation 19

THE CHAPTER OUTLINED:

I. The Marriage of the Lamb in Heaven (19:1-10)
   1. The exposure of the whore
   2. The exaltation of the Bridegroom
   3. The exhibition of the bride

II. The Revelation and the Supper on Earth (19:11-21)
   1. The victorious armies of heaven
   2. The vulturous fowls of the air
   3. The vanquished enemies of the earth

Another literary inset now presents itself for study. In this sense, this chapter is precisely like chapters 7, 10, 11, 12, 13, 14, 17, and 18. All of them were parenthetical in nature, taking up a subject of the story at the point it intruded itself into the narrative and tracing its history backward and forward. This was for the sake of giving the reader full perspective in the understanding of the narrative. Here is the place in the story where the several events of chapter 19 should properly be introduced into the story.

The sequence of events is emphasized by the phrase of verse 1, "after these things." After what things? The answer is after the things of chapters 17 and 18. In those chapters the entire future history of Babylon was charted from beginning to end. The double aspect of the city was discussed. The religious aspect of the city was narrated in chapter 17, and the reader was carried along to the final doom of the harlot at the hands of Antichrist and the ten kings in the midst of the tribulation week (17:16-17). The political aspect of the city was traced through the last three and one-half years of the tribulation in chapter 18 to a point near the close when the immediate judgment of God fell upon it (18:8). After these things the events of chapter 19 take place.

But the time element must be carefully studied in relation to chapters 17 and 18. The first eight verses of chapter 19 relate to both the religious and political aspects of the city of Babylon. After the destruction of the great false religious system centered in this city (v. 2), and after the city of Babylon itself is utterly demolished (v. 3), then the marriage of the Lamb takes place in heaven (19:4-8). The marriage itself, therefore, will take place very near the end of the last three and one-half years of the tribulation period. By this time both the religious system and the center of its operation will have been destroyed.

The marriage supper is properly associated with the marriage (v. 9). But it does not take place in the house of the bride, but rather in the house of the bridegroom. So this event as mentioned in relation to the marriage does not actually occur chronologically until Christ brings the bride to his own house. This means that it will not occur until Christ returns to the earth and sets up the kingdom. Though mentioned in the narrative before the supper recorded in verse 17, it does not occur until later.

The last half of chapter 19 must be associated with the political aspect of Babylon in the sense that its inhabitants are now destroyed (vv. 11-21). The beast and his immediate followers who inhabited the city are destroyed at the coming of Christ. At Christ's coming in glory the Antichrist is defeated and the kings of the earth with their hordes suffer destruction.

At His coming Christ finds them gathered in the valley of Jehoshaphat laying siege to the city of Jerusalem (Zech. 14:1-4). It is this coming of Christ that brings the tribulation period to its end.

This chapter constitutes a brief and swift resume of events that will occur at the very end of the age. The details are treated elsewhere in the Bible. As possible some reference will be made to those in the course of the exposition.

I. THE MARRIAGE OF THE LAMB IN HEAVEN (19:1-10)

The events now being studied take place shortly *after* the judgment of the great whore and the city of Babylon proper (17:16-17; 19:1-3). Since the whore was destroyed in the middle of the week, these events occur some time near the close of the last three and one-half years of tribulation. From the day sin entered into the world through Adam, Satan has been preparing a false bride. False religion everywhere has made the claim to be genuine, supernatural, and godly. Millions have been deceived and led into it. After the true church is caught away to heaven, the false church will make its greatest effort to deceive the millions of earth with the political and commercial aid of Antichrist. During the first three and one-half years of tribulation, it will become one vast, universal system and organization.

The very union and unity of this system of the end time will achieve its desired end. The true church is now gone from the earth. The worldwide organization of the whore will convince millions of her claims. But in that moment when it appears that she has deceived everyone, Satan, who desires worship for only himself and his masterpiece, the Antichrist, will turn on the filthy whore and utterly destroy her. The agelong triangle will then be brought to an end. It will then become evident that the great whore was making a claim to which she had no right. When once the false bride has been exposed, the time will have arrived for the marriage of the Lamb to the true bride.

The city of Babylon too must be destroyed, not only because it was the center of this false religious system, but also because it served as the center for that object of worship which supplanted the harlot, namely, the Antichrist himself. When the false religious system has been exposed and the false object of worship likewise, then has come the time for the marriage of the true church to the true Bridegroom.

In the following ter verses the exposure of the whore is first presented, followed by the exaltation of the Bridegroom, and the section is concluded with the exhibition of the true bride.

1. The exposure of the whore (vv. 1-4). This is greeted with a chorus of "hallelujahs" from heaven. How earnestly the inhabitants of heaven must be following the course of events in the earth! In this respect the earth is really the theater of the universe. The call for heaven to rejoice has already been sounded (18:20), and now the circle of spectators gathered round the throne burst into ecstasies of praise and rejoicing.

(a) An *exclamation* of praise from the great company of the redeemed resounds through heaven (v. 1). The word "alleluia" is exactly the same as the word "hallelujah" and is the Hebrew word meaning "Praise ye the Lord." God should be praised because salvation or deliverance comes from Him, because He is in glory or nature the very essence of holiness, because in honor or value He is precious, and because in power He is able to effect the judgment of the whore.

(b) The *expulsion* of the whore from competition with the true bride is the reason for such praise (v. 2). The judgments of the Lord are true and righteous. The great whore not only committed fornication with the earth, but also shed the blood of the servants of the Lord. The moral corruption in the defilement that was produced in the spirits, minds, and bodies of men, and the physical violence in the deprivation of life constitute two valid reasons for the judgment of God. This judgment followed the lines of righteousness and was true to the facts.

(c) The *extinction* of the whore was deserved, and her punishment is eternal (v. 3). This is another reason for praise. The smoke of the torment of those who comprised this colossal ecclesiastical organization goes up forever as they suffer in the lake of fire. In this sense these people are to be identified with the beast worshipers of chapter 14 (vv. 9-11). Once the false religious system is destroyed by the Antichrist and the ten kings, the devotees of false religion merely transfer their devotion to Antichrist. Since they are victims of strong delusion because they rejected the truth in Christ, their transfer of devotion to Antichrist differs in degree but not in kind (II Thess. 2:3-12). It is therefore correct to expect that their torment will be eternal.

(d) With *exclamations* of praise the four living creatures and the twenty-four elders join in the anthems of praise (v. 4). With bowed knees and solemn accents these creatures and elders fall before the throne and offer up their paeans of praise to the One who sits upon the throne. Here is the answer for that question that has troubled the saints through the millenniums. How can there be no tears in heaven when the saints know their loved ones in the flesh are in eternal torment? The answer is clear.

Once salvation is complete, the scales fall away from the eyes and the heart is in complete harmony with the laws of heaven. Then all the saints will agree with the judgments of the Lord. They will say, "Praise ye the Lord," and "Amen," so be it.

2. The exaltation of the Bridegroom (vv. 5-7). At this point the one who has been directing the course of events from heaven in anticipation of being joined in wedlock to the true church is exalted.

(a) A *command* for praise to Christ comes direct from the throne (v. 5). This order directed to the servants of God is now proper since the whore has been judged. Small and great are commanded to join in it.

(b) The *obedience* to this command follows immediately (v. 6). The voice of a mighty multitude is heard in unison, like the voice of many waters, and like the voice of deep peals of thunder, rumbling forth hallelujah after hallelujah. The reason for praise is stated: "For the Lord God omnipotent reigneth." Reigning means the exercise of authority. The exercise of authority is manifested in a rebellious society by the subjugation of the rebellious. The "amens" and the "hallelujahs" come from the redeemed when they see this authority being exercised. Since the saints were not able to know the heart of God or to read His mind, they supposed that His grace and longsuffering were to be construed as failure on His part. This delay in the exercise of force upon the wicked produced great concern and deep mystery. But now at last there is no longer delay, "for the Lord God omnipotent reigneth."

(c) The *purpose* of this reverberating praise in the courts of heaven is to honor the deserving person upon whom it is bestowed (v. 7). And best of all it is the marriage of the Lamb that has come. Just before the exhibition of the bride, the great Bridegroom is given the central place of attention.

3. The exhibition of the bride (vv. 7-10). The one great day in the life of a woman is her wedding day. That is the day when she is on exhibition. From then on she loses her identity in her husband because she has willingly identified herself with him. This great day is the day of the Church.

(a) The *preparation* of the bride for marriage is suggested by the words, "And his wife hath made herself ready" (v. 7). This is not to be confused with the marriage supper of verse 9. This probably has reference to the judgment seat of Christ, when all the wrongs of the church will be made right (I Cor. 3:13-15; II Cor. 5:10). This judgment will begin the moment the church is caught away into heaven at the Rapture and will continue through the entire period of the tribulation until the destruction of the city of Babylon. By that time the millions who belong to the church will have been examined, and will have prepared themselves for that ineffable experience of being joined to the Heavenly Bridegroom.

(b) The *provision* for the bride in order that she might be properly prepared for her wedding day is granted to her (v. 8). The thing granted or graced to her is fine linen, clean and white, the proper adornment of a bride for her wedding. This white dress is the righteousness or righteous acts of the saints. This, I think, is the making right of the wrongs of which she was guilty in earth, and the reason she is able to do this is because of the fullness of grace that has been bestowed upon her. What the Church could not do before salvation was complete she will now be able to do. Confession will be made, wrongs will be righted, losses will be suffered, and crowns will be bestowed. And thus the bride will be dressed in holy splendor for the momentous occasion of her presentation to the Lamb (Eph. 5:27).

(c) The *personnel* present at the wedding supper in the house of the Bridegroom are described as "blessed" (v. 9). This word means "born again." All the Old Testament saints will be present to celebrate this event (Luke 13:28-29). Besides these, the tribulation saints will be there for the occasion (Rev. 20:4). Since this takes place at the inauguration of the kingdom, redeemed Israel will be present (Matt. 25:1-13), and saved Gentile nations will also take part (Ps. 45; Matt. 25:31-46). Even the angelic hosts will participate (Heb. 1:6).

(d) The *privilege* of the bride to worship God is suggested by the response of God and the instruction of the angel to John (v. 10). Since Christ is the life, center, subject, everything of prophecy, the study and unfolding of prophecy ought so to enhance the beauty and beneficence of the great Bridegroom that it would humble all belonging to the bride in devotion to Him, and increase their longing for His soon return.

II. THE REVELATION AND THE SUPPER ON EARTH (19:11-21)

The student of this passage must be reminded again of some very important matters. The *sequence* of events for this chapter is marked in the opening verse by the phrase "after these things." Chapter 18 recorded the story of the fall of the city of Babylon, which takes place very near the close of the tribulation period. The coming of Christ in glory recorded in verses 11 to 21 of this chapter comes at the very end of the tribulation.

The *place* where the battle of Armageddon is waged is in the earth, for it is fought by Christ with the beast and the kings and armies of earth (v. 19). While up to this point Christ has been directing all the judgment from heaven, He now comes out of heaven and descends to earth for the purpose of completing the work of judgment and ushering in the kingdom where He will rule and reign throughout all eternity.

The *time* of these events is the very close of the tribulation period. The destruction of the city of Babylon occurs near the close of the tribulation period, but there is still some time intervening before the end. The Antichrist is not mentioned in the defeat and doom of the city, which must mean he was absent when judgment fell. But his defeat does come at the end. Millions of people are left to bemoan the fate of Babylon (Dan. 11:44), but none will be left after Christ's coming except the saints (Matt. 13:42-43).

The *occasion* for this final crisis is the situation in which Antichrist finds himself. His campaign against the Jews who fled into the wilderness has been thwarted (12:15-16). His own capital city has fallen as the result of a direct judgment from God (chap. 18). Only one group of people remain against whom he can vent his wrath, and that is a small band of Jews bottled up in the city of Jerusalem (12:17). So he turns his wrath upon them. He marshals an army from out of all the nations (Zech. 14:1-4) and besieges the city.

The *coming* of Christ in glory is the grand consummation of the tribulation period and brings the timely rescue of the remnant of the Jews in Jerusalem (Zech. 9:14-16; 12:8-10; 14:1-4), to say nothing of relieving the pressure of persecution that has been launched against the Gentile saints on a worldwide scale. In verses 11 to 21 there is the prophetic fulfillment of the entire second Psalm.

1. The victorious armies of heaven (vv. 11-16). No imagination can quite visualize this scene for which all the saints of all the ages have been looking.

(a) The *General, Christ,* leads the armies of heaven (vv. 11-13, 16). The door is opened in heaven, not this time to admit others, but to make way for Christ to return to earth. Again the white horse is seen. But this time no one will be deceived. The one who sits upon this white charger is called Faithful and True. In righteousness does He judge and make war.

His eyes are as a flame of fire, and upon His head are many crowns. He has a name written that is known only to himself. His vesture has been dipped in blood, and His name is the Word of God. On His vesture and on His thigh is written the name "King of Kings and Lord of Lords."

(b) The *soldier saints* compose the armies which follow Christ (v. 14). These armies are mounted on white horses and clothed in fine linen, clean and white. The plural, "armies," suggests several vast companies. While the Old Testament saints and the tribulation saints could accompany the church, it is more than likely that this means the various divisions of the church.

(c) The *campaign equipment* is the strangest thing of all (vv. 15-16). There is just one out of the entire group who is equipped to do battle, and that is the General himself. And even He does not have a carnal, material weapon. Out of His mouth goes a sharp, two-edged sword, which is the Word of God. And with that almighty weapon He smites the nations.

(d) The *warfare methods* of these armies are as strange as their equipment (vv. 11, 15). The basis of the warfare is righteousness. Its swiftness is marked by the use of the sword. The only fighter is the General himself, the armies merely viewing the scene. The inexorableness of the judgment is indicated by the fact that He treads the winepress of the fierceness and wrath of Almighty God.

2. The vulturous fowls of the air (vv. 17-18). Nothing like this has ever taken place before. It is a supper prepared by the great God for the fowls of heaven.

(a) The *invitation* to the supper of the great God is made by an angel standing in the sun (v. 17). With a loud voice he calls all the carrion-eating birds that fly in the midst of heaven to gather together for the feast that is being prepared for them by the great God. While the supper to follow this one is one of joy and rejoicing, this first one will be one of gloom and defeat.

(b) The *menu* being prepared is a banquet made up of the flesh of human beings (v. 18). The flesh of kings, captains, military men, and horses used by them; the flesh of free men, bond men, small men and great men, will be served up for the fowls of heaven. A repulsive, gory carnage of such tremendous proportions will be enacted that nothing like it has ever been seen (cf. 14:19-20). Using the carrion birds to dispose of this rotting mass of flesh is one good way of removing the stench and contamination and preparing for the ushering in of the kingdom.

3. The vanquished enemies of earth (vv. 19-21). In three short verses, disposition is made of Antichrist and his armies.

(a) The *confederacy of nations* under the leadership of Antichrist constitute the enemies of Christ (v. 19). These kings and armies under the beast gather in the valley of Jehoshaphat against Jerusalem (Zech. 14:1-4). Though ultimately against Christ, little do the beast and his vassal kings realize that they will meet Him in person.

(b) The *confinement* of the beast and the false prophet in the lake of fire is the final judgment upon these two accomplices of Satan (v. 20; 20:10). Since these leaders are confirmed in sin, there is no need for waiting until the Great White Throne judgment. Their sin is so enormous and so evident that it is not necessary to hold them over for the Great White Throne judgment at the end of the Millennium. Moreover, an exhibition is made of them before the entire aggregation of mankind which followed them.

(c) The *carnage* produced by the sword from the mouth of Christ includes all those making up the vast armies gathered to do battle (v. 21). This does not extend beyond and include all the followers of the beast in the earth. This remains for the judgment of the nations as described in Matthew 25:31-46.

The Millennium
and the Great White Throne

Revelation 20

THE CHAPTER OUTLINED:

I. The Messiah and His Kingdom (20:1-6)
   1. A perfect spiritual environment is established
   2. A perfect moral environment is established
   3. A perfect physical environment

II. The Devil and the Unsaved Nations (20:7-10)
   1. Satan is loosed out of his prison
   2. Sinful nature remains the same
   3. Swift doom falls

III. The Great White Throne (20:11-15)
   1. The sovereign throne of the Lamb
   2. The summons before the throne
   3. The searching character of this judgment
   4. The sentence inflicted upon the wicked
   5. The nature of punishment is suggested

Every student of the Scriptures can be sure that God has made no mistakes in the movements of His plan through the ages. Chapter 20 of Revelation unfolds in a more detailed fashion the unfolding of these great purposes. The glorious appearing of our Lord and Saviour Jesus Christ at the close of the tribulation period does not finish the plan and purposes of God. Final issues are still in the process of being worked out, and a thousand years must run their course, during which there will be another great movement in the unfolding of the program of the ages.

The Millennium has a very real place in the plan of God. Various attitudes have been taken toward the subject of the Millennium. There are three schools of interpretation in conservative circles. First, there are the premillennialists, who take the position that Christ will come back to earth before the Millennium and actually usher in the thousand-year kingdom. It is the conviction of this writer that this is the Biblical position. It is true, though, that those who hold this position are few in number as compared with the number who hold other positions.

Second, there are the postmillennialists, who argue that Christ will come back at the close of the Millennium. This school contends that things in earth get better and better by the efforts of man through the church until the Millennium is ushered in and runs its course, and then Christ returns. The trend in the world, however, has so obviously gone in the opposite direction that this interpretation is almost dead. Most of those who once held this position no longer believe in any of the eschatology of the Scriptures.

The third position is comparatively old, for it goes back to A.D. 400 to the days of the great Church Father, Augustine. Those who hold this position are called a-millennialists. The word means that there is no Millennium at all. How any reader of the Scriptures can take a position like this is amazing. But the great majority of those who claim to be orthodox and conservative today have moved to or declare that they belong to this class. This is to be explained on the basis of the type of theology they hold and their method of interpreting the Scriptures. One can be very sure that a sort of rabbinical casuistry and an exegetical spiritualizing approach must be made to the Scriptures in order to get any support for this position. Six times in this chapter the words "a thousand years" appears (vv. 2-7). The word "millennium" is the Latin word for a thousand years. So the idea is very clearly present here in this chapter.

During the Millennium God will work out certain great purposes, and after the thousand years have run their course this millennial kingdom will merge into the Eternal State and will go on forever This is made certain by many clear passages in the Word of God (Dan. 2:44; 7:13-14, 27; I Cor. 15:24). The Eternal State is the subject for discussion in the final two chapters of Revelation, so we shall not discuss it here.

Chapter 20 of the Revelation has a threefold purpose. It demonstrates the method by which God will accomplish His original kingdom in the earth. Moreover, it demonstrates that man, even though enjoying a perfect environment, will, without the aid of God, finally bring about his own destruction. And, finally, it demonstrates that the basic need of all men is regeneration, a new life from God, which is effected by the operation of the Holy Spirit. This is known as new birth.

Multitudes of redeemed people will enter the millennial kingdom at its outset. There will be a spiritual aristocracy, the church, who will reign as queen with the ruling monarch, the Lord Jesus Christ. The church will sit in His throne (Rev. 3:21) and will rule and reign with Him over the nations (Rev. 2:26-27). The Old Testament saints and the tribulation saints will also rule in some lesser sense (Rev. 20:4, 6). Great numbers of Israelites will enter the kingdom: the 144,000 (Rev. 14:3-4), those who flee into the wilderness (Rev. 12:6, 13-16), and those who remain in Jerusalem (Rev. 12:17); in some sense Israel will be the head of the nations during the Millennium (Deut. 28:1, 13; Zech. 8:23). Millions of Gentiles saved during the tribulation period will also enter into the kingdom (Matt. 25:31-34). But no unsaved person will enter the kingdom at its outset (Matt. 13:41-43, 49-50; 25:41-46).

Moreover, millions of people will be born physically into the kingdom of saved parents who entered at its outset. This will be a population explosion under the most favorable circumstances (Isa. 60:22; Zech. 8:5). There will be no war (Isa. 2:2-4), no poverty (Isa. 65:21-23), no disease or hazards (Isa. 65:20, 25), no limitation of the length of life (Zech. 8:4). Nevertheless, all these born physically into the kingdom will be sinners by nature and in need of salvation (Isa. 65:20). They will demonstrate their sinful nature in rebellion (Zech. 14:16-19), making it necessary for the king to rule with a rod of iron (Rev. 12:5; 19:15). To meet this need, the outpouring of the Holy Spirit (Joel 2:28-32), the atmosphere of holiness (Zech. 14:20-21), the message of salvation (Isa. 52:7-10), and the ministry of the Jews (Isa. 61:6; Rom. 11:15) will be directed to this end. Millions will be saved in order to populate the Eternal State (Rev. 21:24-26), but there will nevertheless be a vast host, by no means the majority, who will resist the message of the Gospel and the moment divine restrictions are lifted at the end of the Millennium will follow Satan to final destruction (Rev. 20:7-10).

I. THE MESSIAH AND HIS KINGDOM (20:1-6)

In these verses the excuse offered by millions to explain away personal responsibility for sinful nature and sinful deeds is answered with finality. That excuse is poor environment: spiritual, moral, and physical. Though this excuse cannot explain how Adam and Eve sinned in the beginning, through the many years since it has been used over and over again. For this reason man has concentrated his attention in large part upon the improving of his environment. Think of how many organizations have for their purpose that of making the world a better place to live in. Because of his sinful nature, man has never succeeded in making his environment any better. In fact, the very opposite is taking place, and the world has been growing worse and worse (II Tim. 3:13).

But what man has never been able to do, and never will be able to do, God does. At the glorious appearing of Christ, by supernatural power Christ brings in His kingdom with a perfect spiritual, moral, and physical environment. Into this perfect kingdom, children are born of saved parents and live here for the better part of a thousand years. But at the end of the thousand years, when Satan is loosed for a little season, it becomes evident that the old sinful nature which they inherited from their parents is unchanged by this perfect environment, and they join in a mass rebellion against Christ and the saints.

1. A perfect spiritual environment is established by the removal of Satan to the bottomless pit for the entire duration of the Millennium (vv. 1-3). An angel from heaven comes down with the key to the pit and a chain in his hand. This angel is not the one mentioned in 9:1. And the chain is not an iron chain. It is the sort of chain by which a great spirit can be bound. Having bound Satan, he casts him into the pit for one thousand years. This means limitation of sinful activity and segregation from influence of society.

The confinement of Satan in the pit, and thus his removal from the sphere in which he could circulate among men and deceive them, makes it absolutely certain that men cannot blame him for their sinful nature or for their sinful deeds. It is made absolutely certain that there is no spiritual hindrance which will prevent improvement of the old nature.

2. A perfect moral environment is established by placing completely saved people in governmental positions, and by starting the kingdom with a saved society (vv. 4-6).

(a) The *sovereign* of this kingdom is Christ himself (Ps. 2:6-9). He will rule with a rod of iron and no wickedness will be tolerated during His reign (Rev. 12:5; Zech. 14:16-21). The saints of the Old and New Testament and the tribulation saints are resurrected for the purpose of ruling and reigning with Christ (vv. 4, 6). The church reigns as the queen with Christ in His throne (Rev. 2:26-27; 3:21), and in some lesser sense the rest of the resurrected saints belonging to the first resurrection serve as judges and rulers during this period. The unsaved perished at the coming of Christ and went into Hades, where they await the resurrection at the end of the Millennium (v. 5).

(b) Beside this vast array of resurrected saints who make up the society of the kingdom, there are *multitudes of saved Jews* (Rev. 14:3-4; 12:6, 13-17) and *Gentiles* (Matt. 25:31-34) who enter the kingdom. They were saved during the tribulation period and come into the kingdom as saved people, living in the same bodies in which they were saved. They still possess the old Adamic nature, which doubtless will gradually be changed and disappear during the years of the Millennium because they were born again and now live in the presence of the King of kings. But they will give birth to children who will inherit the old, sinful nature.

(c) These *children* will live for hundreds of years in the midst of this perfect moral and social environment. Sin will not be tolerated by the King or His rulers, and the saved society will desire only that which glorifies the King. Holiness will be manifest in every phase of society (Zech. 14:20-21). And those people born into this perfect moral and spiritual atmosphere, with a sinful nature, will not be allowed to pollute the atmosphere, for they will be anticipated in their sin before they are able to perform it. Yet at the end of a thousand years they remain unchanged.

3. A perfect physical environment will also remove any further excuse that men might use to explain away sinful nature and deeds. The Book of Revelation does not say anything about this aspect of the kingdom. We find it here only by implication. However, the Scripture contains ample information on this point. The curse will be lifted from nature (Isa. 11:6-9). The desert will bloom as a rose (Isa. 35). Men will own their own premises and enjoy then (Micah 4:4), and will enter into the fruits of their own toil (Amos 9:11-15). No man will then be able to blame his physical environment for the sin of which he is guilty.

II. THE DEVIL AND THE UNSAVED NATIONS (20:7-10)

Another excuse used by many to explain away personal responsibility for sinfulness is heredity. It has been asserted that good parentage produces good children and poor parentage produces bad children. Therefore, if all people could be reformed, or some method of selectivity for procreation could be adopted, a godly society would be the result. This argument overlooks the fact that all men are sinful by nature and that every individual inherits a sinful nature. During the Millennium children are born of people who were saved, and then after living in a perfect moral and spiritual society for hundreds of years, they turn and follow the great arch deceiver and enemy of God. Here is proof that the old nature is at enmity with God and will not be subject to Him. It is proof that nothing short of new birth will fashion a man for the kingdom of God.

1. Satan is loosed out of his prison for a little season (v. 7). According to verse 3, it is necessary that Satan be loosed for a little season. He is still the same after a thousand years of incarceration. Evil nature does not change merely because it is confined in prison. The nature is fixed, and Satan is determined to follow on in the path he settled upon millenniums before. He started out as the enemy of God, and he intends to pursue this path to his doom (Rev. 12:12). Furthermore, by delaying final judgment upon Satan God is not only able to prove the justice of final judgment, but also to use him yet as the one to demonstrate that sinful human nature after the thousand years under perfect conditions is still the same and must suffer penal judgment.

2. Sinful nature remains the same, as is demonstrated by the fact that unsaved millions follow after Satan (vv. 8-9). Under such favorable conditions as exist during the Millennium the human race multiplies until countless millions of people exist. Satan, now loosed, goes out among them and organizes the greatest rebellion ever known against God. They go up on the breadth of earth and crowd into the land of Palestine. The one object of their hatred is the capital city, the beloved Jerusalem, where the King dwells with His queen and the attendant saints. This horde is bent on the destruction of those under whom they have been compelled to live in righteousness through the Millennium. Except for the immediate intervention of divine justice, Calvary would be acted out all over again.

This is the demonstration of the validity of words spoken to a great teacher in Israel long ago: "Except a man be born again, he cannot see the kingdom of God" (John 3:3). Lying at the root of all the ills of the world is the fallen nature of mankind. For this there is only one cure, and that is the impartation of the life of God himself. This is effected by means of new birth. War, and poverty, and disease, and ignorance are effects of that sinful nature acquired in the fall and passed on to all men by natural generation. Only by means of new birth will the nature of man be so transformed that he can experience the dominion of God. "The carnal mind is enmity against God: for it is not subject to the law of God, neither indeed can be" (Rom. 8:7). Here is the demonstration in this final rebellion against God at the end of the Millennium.

3. Swift doom falls upon those who join in this rebellion (vv. 9-10). Fire comes down from God out of heaven and devours the entire ungodly, uncontrolled, unholy horde. Death takes them into Hades, where they await the resurrection of the wicked. Without further delay Satan is cast into the lake of fire that burns with brimstone, and there, together with his accomplices, his dupes, he is tormented day and night forever and ever. The sentence of judgment for Satan was passed at the cross (John 12:31-33; 16:11), and now it is inflicted. The infliction of the sentence was delayed until God was through using Satan for His own purpose. The hour has dawned for the execution, and without hesitation he is cast into the lake of fire. Hell was planned and prepared for the devil and his angels (Matt. 25:41). Angels which followed him have been confined there for centuries (II Peter 2:4). The beast and the false prophet were sent to this place immediately at the close of the tribulation period and have already suffered for one thousand years (Rev. 20:10).

III. THE GREAT WHITE THRONE JUDGMENT (20:11-15)

Perfect environment has failed men. Natural heredity has failed men. Because men still believe that there is a goodness in men they will stand before the bar of justice, this last excuse is utterly swept away. Before the white throne of God, where the ineffable holiness, righteousness, and justice of God are emphasized, wicked men are now assembled. Here absolute justice will be meted out to them. Rejection of the Son of God and His work on Calvary placed them in the group of the lost. Now they will be judged for the works they have committed, and the degree of punishment they deserve will be inflicted upon them.

1. The sovereign throne of the Lamb (v. 11). This is not the throne of Revelation 4:2 in one sense. That was a throne in white encircled by a rainbow. The aspect of whiteness was then tempered with color, pointing to mercy in the midst of judgment. But now there is nothing to relieve the awful whiteness of the throne. This means that the time of salvation is past. At this throne, no grace will be shown, no love, no mercy, no pity. Here the solemn justice of the infinite God will be executed.

Christ is the one who sits on this throne. All judgment has been committed to Him (John 5:22), for He is a Son of man (John 5:27). No one is more qualified than He for this task. He first did all He could do to rescue men from eternal doom. When at last the wicked come before Him, they will recognize the one whom they rejected, and they will be speechless. The awesomeness of this throne is so great that even the earth and the heaven flee away in horror.

2. The summons before the throne goes forth to the wicked dead (vv. 12-13). The voice of the Son of God calls all the dead to judgment (John 5:28-29). Those who are in the grave are the wicked. They are the ones who share in this final resurrection. Death, which stands for the physical experience of all, gives up the bodies; and hell (Hades, ASV) yields up the souls and spirits of men. Then the bodies and the souls and spirits are joined together for judgment. These bodies are no more changed than the souls that inhabit them. Since they sinned under these circumstances and rejected Christ in these bodies, they now must face the Saviour they rejected and be judged in the same bodies in which they sinned.

3. The searching character of this judgment is marked by the books present at the bar of justice (vv. 12-13). God keeps books, and His books are absolutely accurate. The book of life is present, and it is open. No one at this bar of justice dares find fault with the Judge, arguing that they do not belong at this throne. There is the book of life, and their names do not appear in that book. But that is their fault, for by grace their names could have been written there. In the other books are recorded the deeds they performed while living in the earth. Some have more guilt recorded against them than do others. The motive, means, and result of each work are looked at by the Judge. All had a selfish motive, refusing to give glory to God or accept the Son. Many used evil means to accomplish their deeds. Few indeed actually did anything that had a good result. But God is just, and this is a throne of justice. The sentence decreed upon each one will be determined by the degree of his wickedness.

4. The sentence inflicted upon the wicked consists of various degrees of punishment in the lake of fire (vv. 14-15). All must go to the lake of fire and suffer the second physical death. There will then be no need for a Hades to receive the soul and death to claim the body. Both are cast into the lake of fire. The fire consumes the body, and the soul and spirit go out unclothed to suffer the degree of punishment deserved (Luke 12:47-48). This punishment is divine in origin, for it is God who inflicts it (Luke 12:5; Heb. 10:27, 30-31; 12:29). It is eternal in duration, for there the fire is not quenched (Matt. 25:46; Mark 9:44). And this punishment is excruciating in character, for their worm dieth not (Mark 9:44). Ceaselessly the memory taunts the soul for failure to heed the call of the Saviour (Luke 16:24-31).

5. The nature of punishment is suggested by one verse in the Epistle of James. It reads, "The tongue is a fire . . . and it is set on fire of hell" (James 3:6). One thing is true, it is not a material fire, nor is it set on fire by material fire. It is the fire in the human spirit that sets the tongue on fire. If this be true, then perhaps here is the explanation; the sinful human spirit grows in its character and development throughout the lifetime of a man. When at the second death there comes the separation of the body from the spirit by consumption of the body in material flames, then the spirit goes out without any body as a vehicle through which to express itself. All those sinful passions that once had a body through which to give expression must now burn on and on without ever being expressed. This sort of torture would certainly be according to one's works.

New Jerusalem, the Lamb of God, and Eternity

Revelation 21 and 22

THE CHAPTER OUTLINED:

I. The Establishment of Eternal Blessedness (21:1-8)
1. The presence of the final order
2. The provision for the final order
3. Certain things are prevented from entering this new order

II. The Exhibition of Eternal Blessedness (21:9-27)
1. The descending of the holy city, New Jerusalem, is now exhibited to John
2. The description of the city follows
3. The delights of the Holy Jerusalem will be felt by all the nations of earth

III. The Experience of Eternal Blessedness (22:1-5)
1. The river of water of life
2. The tree of life
3. The Throne of God and of the Lamb
4. The face of the Lamb
5. The light of the world

IV. The Exhortation Based on Eternal Blessedness (22:6-21)
1. The importance of these things
2. The invitation
3. The inviolability of these things

The sequence of events is clearly marked by phrases occurring in chapters 20 and 21. The Millennium has now run its course and is finished (20:3, 5, 7). The final stage of things is now ushered in and will continue forever. There is no reason why chapters 21 and 22 should not be regarded as describing something which follows the Millennium. The paragraph beginning with verse 11 of chapter 20 continues without break right on through verse 8 of chapter 21. The Great White Throne fixed the destiny of all the wicked. Death and Hades are merged with the lake of fire.

The change of scenes is important to the understanding of these chapters. The one who sits on the throne declares, "Behold, I make all things new" (21:5). The verb is in the present tense and suggests the progressive accomplishment of this task. With the ushering in of the Millennium this was begun. Following the Great White Throne judgment this task was completed. The earth and the heaven fled away and a new heaven and earth have taken their place (20:11; 21:1), so that the former things have all disappeared (21:4). The state of the sinful is fixed for eternity (20:10; 21:8), and so also is the state of the righteous (22:5).

The conditions of the Eternal State are now brought to the place of absolute perfection. The kingdom of our Lord and Saviour Jesus Christ was a perfect kingdom in every respect except for the fact that righteousness did not yet dwell in it as it will in the new heavens and the new earth (II Peter 3:13). For this reason, after the wicked nations and their satanic leader are finally dispatched, a great conflagration produced by God, in which the old order of things is completely changed, will usher in a new heaven and a new earth (II Peter 3:10-13; Rev. 21:1). This does not mean that the heavens and earth which are now will be blotted out of existence. It merely means that there will be a complete arrangement of things, with every evidence of the sinful order removed, and a new order and arrangement made which will be the proper abode and dwelling place for righteousness.

The purpose for this change is that the kingdom of Christ may merge with the Eternal State and go right on (Dan. 2:44; 7:14, 18, 22, 27). This will be the time when the kingdom is handed over to the Father that God might be all and in all (I Cor. 15:24-28). This will be carried out in order that the final order may be made forever permanent (Heb. 12:25-27). This portion of Scripture is given to show men that what God started out to accomplish in the beginning here in the earth He is now bringing to completion. It was God's intention to dwell in the earth with men forever in perfect fellowship and communion. At last this great plan is achieved, and

New Jerusalem descends to earth where Christ will dwell with His bride in the presence of men, and all nations will worship Him as the Lamb who redeemed them and produced this state of perfection and bliss. Seven times in the course of these chapters Christ is referred to as the Lamb (21:9, 14, 22-23, 27; 22:1, 3). The loving devotion shown to Him throughout eternity will be the complete realization of God's place and purpose in redemption (Eph. 1:5-6, 12, 14; John 17:24).

I. THE ESTABLISHMENT OF ETERNAL BLESSEDNESS (21:1-8)

The stage is now set for all eternity. There is the presence of the final order of things, the necessary provision for that order, and the things prohibited from entering that order.

1. The presence of the final order (vv. 1-4) is marked by the passing of the old order (v. 1), the presence of the bride (v. 2), the presence of the Lord (v. 3), and the passing of the effects of sin (v. 4). As far as the Book of Revelation is concerned, there is no good reason why these things should not be taken literally. The first heaven and earth have passed away, and a new heaven and earth have taken their place. The word "new" does not mean new in substance, but new in arrangement. Not one molecule or atom of the first order will cease to exist, but they will all be rearranged so that the effects of sin will disappear. Undoubtedly there will be such a tremendous rearrangement of the earth's surface that there will be no more seas or oceans to separate men and deprive them of three-fourths of the earth's surface. Perhaps irrigation of the earth will be by the method in Eden (Gen. 2:6). Population increase that has troubled men for centuries will no longer exist. When three-fourths of the earth's surface is restored for habitation, and the other one-fourth is not only made to blossom as the rose, but made fertile a thousand times over, it will be inconceivable how great a population the earth will be able to support.

The holy city, new Jerusalem, prepared in heaven for the bride of Christ as her eternal dwelling place with Christ, will descend to earth (John 14:1-3; Rev. 21:2). There are some who insist strongly that the city will be suspended above the earth. But the easiest reading of the text suggests that it rests upon the earth. In this city Christ will dwell among men displaying His glory in His bride and in himself for the blessing of the nations. He will be their God and dwell with them, and the nations of earth will be His people (v. 3). Every evidence of the former order will be completely done away (v. 4). No more sin, sorrow, suffering, tears of crying, no more pain or death will be there. John finds it almost impossible to describe this new order without pointing out that things are not like the old order. It seems easier to describe the new order by pointing out from the negative side what it will not be like. This is true because men are more familiar with the present conditions of a sinful order.

2. The provision for the final order (vv. 5-7) rests entirely in the Lord Jesus Christ himself. It is Christ who sits upon the throne, and He is the one who has made all things new. He began this work at His second coming, and He has now brought it to a close. It is done. Let every one realize that these words are true and faithful, for they are uttered by one who is the Alpha and Omega, that is, the A to Z in wisdom, and is the beginning and the end, namely, the one who originated everything and in whom everything will reach its grand consummation. Christ cannot resist another blessed invitation to anyone who will take of the water of life which He offers without money and without price. For those who have drunk deeply at the fountain of life, one evidence will be a life of victory. This is his credential for inheriting everything and, best of all, his right to sweet, blessed fellowship with the eternal God in Christ.

3. Certain things are prevented from entering this new order (v. 8). Since absolute holiness and righteousness are to characterize the new order, mere sentiment cannot be the deciding factor for what shall enter this new order. Holiness decrees that the portion of the fearful, the unbelieving, the abominable, the murderers, the fornicators, the sorcerers, the idolaters, and all liars shall be in the lake of fire. To allow them to enter the new order would be to plant the seeds that would destroy the new heavens and the new earth. They must suffer the second death, which is separation from God, from the earth, and from heaven.

II. THE EXHIBITION OF ETERNAL BLESSEDNESS (21:9-27)

1. The descending of the holy city, New Jerusalem, is now exhibited to John (vv.9-10). The word "shew," appearing twice in these verses, means a great public demonstration. From a high mountain John sees this city descending to the earth. From the standpoint of the people in it, it is the Lamb's wife. From the standpoint of the place, it is the holy Jerusalem, that great city which Christ has built and which will be located in the earth. It is the city for which Abraham looked (Heb. 11:10), for which the saints have looked (Heb. 11:16), and which Christ promised (John 14:1-3).

2. The description of the city follows (vv. 11-23). This is a real city in which the Bridegroom will dwell with His perfected bride, the church

(Eph. 5:27; John 14:3). Every detail should be taken literally. Men build cities out of brick and mortar and stone. But God is the builder of this city and He has everything necessary to build a real palace. Everything in this city speaks of something about the glories and virtues of God, indicating that the materials serve a twofold purpose: (1) They are the substance of construction, and (2) they provide symbolism for contemplation.

(a) The *effulgence* of the city is "the glory of God" (vv. 11, 23). It is the holiness of the Son of God that gives light to it. And hence there is no need for sun, moon, or stars, though they exist. This glory ever reminds men that "God is light, and in him is no darkness at all" (I John 1:5), that the supreme and central thing about God is His holiness (Isa. 6:3).

(b) The *entrance* to the city is captivating (vv. 12-13, 21). Angels are at the twelve gates, and upon these gates are the names of the twelve tribes of Israel to remind the saints that "salvation is of the Jews" (John 4:22). Each gate is made of pearl, the formation of which in the side of an oyster is a token of the fact that it took the death of the Lamb to provide a way of entrance into this city. The angels are God's ministers assisting the saints to arrive at this blessed destination in the holy city (Heb. 1:13-14).

(c) The *foundations* of the city are made of precious stones (vv. 14, 19-20). The names of the twelve apostles appear there to remind the church that it is built upon those men (Eph. 2:20).

(d) The *magnitude* of the city is beyond comparison (vv. 15-16). If it is not a cube fifteen hundred miles in each direction, then it is a pyramid fifteen hundred miles square and fifteen hundred miles high. Christ, the chief cornerstone, will appear at the top (Eph. 2:20) and be the light of the city. No one but God could build a city like this. Anything that man has ever conceived will fade into insignificance. It will be seen even towering over the works of man and reminding him that the supernatural and the infinite are present in Him who is the supreme object of worship.

(e) The *enclosure* of the city consists of a wall made of jasper, clear as crystal, like diamond (vv. 17-18). It glows with whiteness, reminding one of the glory of God (vv. 11, 23), and in this wall lie protection and privacy for the bride of the Lamb and for the inhabitants of the universe.

(f) The *material* of the city is pure gold (vv. 18, 21). Its buildings are pure gold, so crystalline that it is like glass. And the streets are paved with it. This transparent material throws back and forth and into the surrounding regions the brightness of the glory of God like scintillating facets. In this the saints are reminded that the holiness of God is the foundation for every blessing, the environment for every joy, the illumination for every beauty.

(g) The *worship* of the city gathers about the person of the Lord Jesus Christ (vv. 22-23). The Tabernacle in the wilderness and the Temple of the city of Jerusalem were made to symbolize everything that is in Christ. But no temple is needed in this city, for the Lord Jesus Christ, the image of the invisible God made flesh, is its temple. All mankind can look upon His face and behold His glory. Symbols and signs and sacraments and systems of worship will be done away forever. All those things that have produced division, difference, and distress because men have been unable to see them from the same viewpoint will be unnecessary. Men can look immediately upon the object of their worship, for Christ is the temple.

3. The delights of the Holy Jerusalem will be felt by all the nations of earth (vv. 24-27).

Salvation will be one of the blessings felt by the nations that walk in the light of this city (v. 24). Not only do these nations enjoy salvation themselves, but the light of salvation which throws its beam far out across the world will continually evoke the amazement of mankind.

Sanctification will be another direct result felt by the nations (v. 24). They will "walk" and "keep on walking" in the light of this city.

A *satisfaction* and freedom will be felt by mankind in relation to this city (v. 25). The gates will always be open. No night ever comes to this city. The luminaries in the sky and the rotation of the earth bring day and night. But the Lamb is in this city, and He is the light exceeding even the brilliance of the midday sun. There is never any occasion when it is necessary to close the gates against the inhabitants of the night. Men may come and go at will. And the greatest of joy will be felt by the unending stream of pilgrims who come to the city to see the King and His bride.

Separation from all wicked creatures and things will be another one of the delights (v. 27). Sin and sinners will be banished forever. Since sin is always associated with persons, those who defile, work abomination, or make a lie have been sent to their own place, and this city is reserved for those whose names, thanks be to God for His marvelous grace, are written in the Lamb's book of life.

How indescribably appropriate it is that the nations should bring their *salutations* into this city (vv. 24, 26). The saved nations of earth will do wondrous things in those days, and with true hearts single to the glory of God will bring their glory and honor into the city to give due recognition to Him who made their success possible.

The significance of the nations and the location of the New Jerusalem produce deep interest in all those who take seriously the message of this book. If the reader were to approach this book with no preconceived ideas and no theological bias, he would almost certainly conclude that these nations are comprised of saved people living in the flesh, as was true of Adam and Eve before the fall. They live and work in an absolutely sinless society. Since there is no sin, there is no death. And there is no reason why life should not be lived in the flesh in endless perpetuity. Whether there is propagation, there is no word upon which to hazard even speculation.

Assuming that this is true concerning the nations of mankind, it seems quite plausible that the New Jerusalem should rest directly upon the earth. Since there are no seas, there is no problem of room for its location. It provides a center for all the nations of earth. It is here that the supreme object of worship is located. It is here that the supreme government is centralized. It is here that the nations can come to display the works of their hands to the King and pay their homage and devotion to God. In and out of the city an endless stream of pilgrims make their journey.

III. THE EXPERIENCE OF ETERNAL BLESSEDNESS (22:1-5)

Here again the imagery is literal. There are a real river, tree, throne, face, and light in this celestial city that now is located in the earth. In each one of these things there is a constant reminder of the grace of God that is being experienced by men.

1. **The river of water of life** is a constant reminder of their regeneration when the Holy Spirit of God came to dwell in them, and continues to dwell in them providing them with all the luxury of the very nature of God (v. 1). This water comes direct from the throne of God and the Lamb, as does the Holy Spirit.

2. **The tree of life**, once in the garden of Eden, now flourishes in the streets of the city and on either side of the river. Its fruitage is through every month of the year. There is plenty for the nations. It is a constant reminder of God's provision and preservation by grace (v. 2).

3. **The Throne of God and of the Lamb** banishes the curse upon the earth and arouses an everlasting devotion and service from the nations. That throne is not only the symbol of sovereignty, but it is also the source of the grace and goodness and blessing that humbled the nations before it.

4. **The face of the Lamb** glows in brilliance surpassing the brightness of the sun (v. 4). The very vision of that face imprints His name upon the foreheads of all men. Its dignity, splendor, preeminence, and grace make

men stand in awe, and wonder, and gratitude for Him (v. 4).

5. The light of the world is now the glory of God that shines in the face of Jesus Christ (II Cor. 4:6). No night can exist in His presence. No candle is needed in the most remote corner. And even the sun appears like a distant and fading star. And those saints to whom the task of reigning has been committed will carry on their task for ever and ever (v. 5).

IV. THE EXHORTATION BASED ON ETERNAL BLESSEDNESS (22:6-21)

The grand story has come to an end, but the blessings await fulfillment, and once begun they will never end. Only one thing remains for John to do, and that is to impress the reader with the importance of this message.

1. The importance of these things is clearly indicated by several things said about them (vv. 6-11). In the first place, these things are *faithful and true* (vv. 6-7). They are true in that they are statements of fact. They are faithful in that they will surely come to pass. The sending of an angel to announce these things indicates the urgency of the message, and the statement of Christ that He is coming quickly should arouse men to act upon them.

In the second place, these things are *fearful* (vv. 8-9). John was constrained to fall before the angel and worship, but the angel insisted that he should worship God.

In the third place, these things are *final* (vv. 10-11). This book should not be sealed, for the time is at hand. Any moment these things may begin to come to pass. And when they do, no more opportunity will be extended to men to change.

2. The invitation is again extended to men to accept these blessed truths and thus be ready for the day when they come to pass (vv. 12-17). *Reward* is held out as an incentive for men to grasp the truth and live by it. And Christ seals this with His own blessed person (v. 13). The *right* and privilege to participate in the blessings of intimate fellowship of the city, while outside the unsaved are in darkness and suffering, should be an inducement to keep the commandments of God (vv. 14-15, ASV). The *reality* of blessings never known by the multitudes of lost men and women is announced by Christ (vv. 16-17). Their reality is emphasized by a series of invitations coming from the Spirit and the bride. And the Lord Jesus urges the one who hears to come, and invites the man who feels his deep thirst.

3. The inviolability of these things is recorded in the closing words to warn men who may deny their truth in their own minds, or who may go so far as to try to change the record (vv. 18-21). A sentence is pronounced upon that person who dares to alter the record (vv. 18-19). Those who alter the record retreat from reality and imperil their own souls. For instance, the suddenness of Christ's coming may possibly catch such a person in the very act of changing the record. Christ himself declares that He may come quickly, and John joins Him with a prayer to come quickly (v. 20). The *seal* upon this entire book and all believers who read and keep the message is the grace of God (v. 21) and the name "Amen" (Rev. 3:14).

CONCLUSION

The greatest story ever written has now come to an end. It has an end not because the facts reach a termination, but because time and space and human energy for recording the facts are exhausted. Nevertheless, all of the essential facts are present. For that person groping his way through the darkness, there is enough light to illumine his path into the very courts of heaven. And for that one who reads and rejects, this same message will rise up in the day of judgment against him.

Books on Revelation
for further study

For the reader's further study, the author has listed a number of excellent books and commentaries on Revelation.

Barnhouse, Donald Grey. *Revelation: God's Last Word.* Grand Rapids: Zondervan Publishing House, 1971.

Cohen, Gary C. *Understanding Revelation.* Collingswood, N. J.: Christian Beacon Press, 1968.

Cohen, Gary C., and Kirban, Salem. *Revelation Visualized.* Chicago: Moody Press, 1972.

Ironside, H. A. *Lectures on the Book of Revelation.* New York: Loizeaux Brothers, 1930.

Larkin, Clarence. *Book of Revelation.* Philadelphia: Published by the Author, 1919.

Lindsey, Hal. *There's a New World Coming.* Santa Ana, Calif.: Vision House Publishers, 1973.

LeHaye, Tim F. *Revelation.* Grand Rapids: Zondervan Publishing House, 1974.

McGee, J. Vernon. *Reveling Through Revelation.* 2 Vols. Los Angeles: Church of the Open Door, n.d.

Meyer, Nathan M. *From Now To Eternity.* Winona Lake, Ind.: BMH Books, 1976.

Morgan, G. Campbell. *The Letter of Our Lord.* Westwood, N. J.: Fleming H. Revell Co., n.d.

Newell, William R. *The Book of the Revelation.* Chicago: Moody Press, 1935.

Phillips, John. *Exploring Revelation.* Chicago: Moody Press, 1974.

Ryrie, Charles Caldwell. *Revelation.* Chicago: Moody Press, 1972.

Seiss, Joseph A. *Lectures on the Apocalypse.* Grand Rapids: Zondervan Publishing House, 1957.

Smith, J. B. *A Revelation of Jesus Christ.* Scottdale, Pa., Herald Press, 1961.

Strauss, Lehman. *The Book of the Revelation.* Neptune, N. J.: Loizeaux Brothers, 1964.

Tenney, Merrill C. *Interpreting Revelation.* Grand Rapids: William B. Eerdmans Publishing Co., 1957.

Walvoord, John F. *The Revelation of Jesus Christ.* Chicago: Moody Press, 1966.

ABOUT THE AUTHOR –

Dr. Herman A. Hoyt is President Emeritus of Grace College and
Grace Theological Seminary, Winona Lake, Indiana. He graduated
valedictorian from Ashland College (A.B.) and *summa cum laude*
from Ashland Theological Seminary (B.Th.). He earned his B.D.,
Th.M. and Th.D. degrees at Grace Theological Seminary. In addition
to books on church polity and the new birth, he has written on
Romans, Hebrews, Revelation and the End Times.

DEMONS, EXORCISM AND THE EVANGELICAL. By Dr. John J. Davis, executive vice president of Grace Schools. An enlightening discussion of demons as personal beings, the practice of exorcism, and an answer to the question: "Can believers be possessed?"

IS THE UNITED STATES IN PROPHECY? By Dr. Herman A. Hoyt, president emeritus of Grace Schools. This booklet reveals answers to questions many people have been asking.

DOES GOD WANT CHRISTIANS TO PERFORM MIRACLES TODAY? By Dr. John C. Whitcomb, professor of theology and Old Testament at Grace Theological Seminary. An analysis of today's faith healers and miracle workers.

DID CHRIST DIE ONLY FOR THE ELECT? By Dr. Charles R. Smith, associate professor of Greek and theology at Grace Theological Seminary. A scholarly and logical treatment of questions regarding the limited atonement and human responsibilities.

A CAPSULE VIEW OF THE BIBLE. By W. Russell Ogden, pastor of the First Brethren Church, Lanham, Maryland. A unique booklet enabling the reader to grasp an overview of the contents of the Bible. Ideal for the individual who desires to see the Bible as a whole unit.

CAN YOU KNOW GOD'S WILL FOR YOUR LIFE? By Dr. Charles R.

Smith. A fresh and informative guide to help the reader determine and have assurance regarding the will of God for his or her life.

CHRIST, OUR PATTERN AND PLAN. By Dr. John C. Whitcomb. An analysis of evangelical missions and evangelism in the light of the great commission.

All booklets in this Contemporary Theological Discussion Series are 16 pages, paperback, and priced at 50c each. Available at your local Christian bookstore or by mail from BMH Books, P. O. Box 544, Winona Lake, Ind. 46590. (Special offer — all seven of the above for $3.25; postage paid when your check accompanies the order.)

ADDITIONAL STUDY GUIDES IN THIS SERIES . . . .

DEUTERONOMY, Bernard N. Schneider, paper, $2.95.

JOSHUA, JUDGES & RUTH, John J. Davis, paper, $2.95.

I & II SAMUEL & I KINGS 1-11, John J. Davis, paper, $2.95.

KINGS & CHRONICLES, John C. Whitcomb, cloth, $3.95; paper, $2.95.

PROVERBS, Charles W. Turner, paper, $2.95.

GOSPEL OF JOHN, Homer A. Kent, Jr., cloth, $3.95; paper, $2.95.

ACTS, Homer A. Kent, Jr., paper, $2.95.

ROMANS, Herman A. Hoyt, paper, $2.95.

I CORINTHIANS, James L. Boyer, cloth, $3.95; paper, $2.95.

GALATIANS, Homer A. Kent, Jr., paper, $2.95.

EPHESIANS, Tom Julien, paper, $2.95.

PHILIPPIANS, David L. Hocking, paper, $2.95.

I & II TIMOTHY, Dean Fetterhoff, paper, $2.95.

HEBREWS, Herman A. Hoyt, paper, $2.50.

JAMES, Roy R. Roberts, paper, $3.50.

I, II, III JOHN, Raymond E. Gingrich, paper, $2.95.

REVELATION, Herman A. Hoyt, paper, $2.95.

THE WORLD OF UNSEEN SPIRITS, Bernard N. Schneider, paper, $2.95.

PROPHECY, THINGS TO COME, James L. Boyer, paper, $2.95.

*Order from your local Christian bookstore or BMH Books,
P. O. Box 544, Winona Lake, IN 46590. (Include a check
with your order and BMH Books pays all postage charges.)*